WHITE
WINES
of the
WORLD

Also by Sheldon Wasserman

THE WINES OF ITALY

Also by Sheldon Wasserman and Pauline Wasserman

THE WINES OF THE CÔTES DU RHÔNE
DON'T ASK YOUR WAITER

WHITE WINES
of the
WORLD

Sheldon and Pauline
Wasserman

STEIN AND DAY/*Publishers*/New York

First published in 1978
Copyright © 1978 by Sheldon Wasserman and Pauline Wasserman
ALL RIGHTS RESERVED
Designed by Tere LoPrete
PRINTED IN THE UNITED STATES OF AMERICA
Stein and Day/*Publishers*/Scarborough House, Briarcliff Manor, N.Y. 10510

Library of Congress Cataloging in Publication Data
Wasserman, Sheldon.
    White wines of the world.

    1. Wine and wine making,   I. Wasserman, Pauline,
joint author. II. Title.
TP548.W34   641.2′2   77-16661
ISBN 0-8128-2461-X

To Dr. Konstantin Frank,
the first man
to grow the fine European (vinifera)
grape varieties successfully
in the northeastern United States,
in appreciation for all he has done
to improve the quality of wine in the United States

Contents

Acknowledgments

In writing this book we have been assisted in various ways by a number of people who have been very helpful, and we would like to take this opportunity to express our appreciation.

Our thanks to Charles Fournier for offering helpful information and for his splendid introduction to this book.

Our thanks also to Robert Gourdin and to Carlo Russo for their encouragement and helpful suggestions.

To numerous winemakers in the United States and Europe who provided information and the opportunity to taste a variety of wines. We especially would like to express our appreciation to Dr. Konstantin Frank of Hammondsport, N.Y.; Comte Lafon (Meursault) and André Gagey (of Louis Jadot) of Burgundy; Anne and André Brunel (Les Cailloux, Chateauneuf-du-Pape), André Canet (Château Grillet), and Max Chapoutier of the Côtes du Rhône; Angelo Papagni, Bruce Herman (Mirassou Vineyards), and Ed Ringsbridge (Veedercrest) of California; Ned Kelley (Frederick Wildman); and Walter Taylor (Bully Hill Winery) who were especially helpful.

To Bernie Fradin who offered encouragement and helpful suggestions.

To Charles Castelli who poured some fine bottles.

And to Tom Abruzzini who did the same; for his invaluable suggestions and information on Italian white wines.

To Patrice Gourdin who afforded opportunities to taste numerous white wines.

To Harry Foulds who also gave encouragement and useful suggestions, not to mention his assistance back home while we were off in the vineyards gathering information.

We would also like to thank any others who helped in any way and deserve acknowledgment but whose names may have been inadvertently omitted.

WHITE
WINES
of the
WORLD

Introduction

The wine business in America has been growing substantially every year for the past ten years, and there have been a lot of books published on all of the aspects of wine.

However, a great number of Americans still have only a limited knowledge of the great number of varieties of wines and wine districts of the world. This book will help to fill this void. It presents a very concise nomenclature of wine districts, vineyards, and wine terms in a style that is very clear and easy to understand.

Sheldon Wasserman has many qualifications to do such a job and has done it exceedingly well.

He has gathered his wide knowledge of wine by traveling to the important wine districts of the world, visiting many vineyards and wineries, and by being involved with the American groups who are doing a big job of promoting the use of wine in the United States. His wife, Pauline, is also a wine connoisseur in her own right and has always been Sheldon's associate in all his endeavors.

Both of them, together or separately, have already published several great books. Furthermore, their books and articles have been consumer oriented. Sheldon's book, *The*

Wines of Italy, is very complete, easy to read, and will give the readers a clear understanding of the various wines of that sunny country.

It has been, and is, my privilege to have known both of them for some time, and I am sure that their latest effort will be one more step in the increased wine appreciation of Americans.

CHARLES FOURNIER
Honorary Lifetime President & Consultant
Gold Seal Vineyards

Why White Wine?

More and more Americans are discovering wine, particularly white wine. Increasingly, Americans are asking for a glass of white wine in place of a cocktail. Having white wine with lunch or with dinner. Sipping a cool glass of white wine in the afternoon. What is behind this rise in popularity? Why white wine?

White wines appeal in a number of aspects. They are easy to serve. They require little or no aging. They are drunk cold. They are available in a wide range of styles. They tend to be lighter in alcohol than many other drinks. They go with any type of food. They can be enjoyed alone, without food, or as an aperitif. And they are very pleasant drinking. White wines do have a lot going for them.

They're almost as easy to serve as they are to drink. They require little preparation—just chill, open, and pour. There is no problem of mixing as with cocktails. There is no problem of timing—opening the bottle in advance to give the wine air, as with the red wines, which can take as much as several hours of air depending on the wine. This can be a bit of a bother to most people. Chilling is really the only preparation a white wine requires. And if the bottle isn't already in the refrigerator when needed, it can simply be popped into an ice bucket filled with cubes and ice water for speedy chilling.

White wines are ready to drink. They don't require being put aside to age before they are ready, or enjoyable, to drink. Yes, a noble Chardonnay or Riesling, a great Burgundy, Sauternes, or Auslese will improve dramatically in bottle, but they can be enjoyed in their youth as well. Red wines, by comparison, can be harsh, tannic, and astringent when young, requiring years in bottle to smooth out and mellow.

Most red wines are best at cool room temperature, but white wines are best drunk chilled. As most Americans drink their beverages either cold or hot but not in between, a cold wine has refreshing appeal. It's a delightful thirst quencher.

Wine is the natural, traditional, beverage with food. White wines go with any dish. Serving becomes simple, while dinner becomes something special. While some foods go better with red wine than with white wine, there are no dishes that match only with reds and clash with whites. And because of the diversity in white wines, a white wine can be found to go with any dish that can go with a red. The same is not true of red wines. Something in the flavor of fish, for example, clashes with the tannin in red wine. And while venison or beef might overpower a white wine, the flavors don't clash.

White wines are made in the widest range of styles—from bone-dry, light-bodied, delicate wines to lusciously sweet, full-bodied dessert wines. This makes it easy to find one for every taste.

While they go well with food, white wines don't require food to be enjoyed. In fact, some white wines—notably the great German Rieslings from the Mosel or the Rheingau—are best by themselves. Food, in these cases, seems to get in the way. Red wines are food wines; they really require at least a bit of bread or cheese to be enjoyed. Even a light, fresh, fruity Beaujolais seems to lack something when drunk alone. Some whites are better with food, but many are quite enjoyable drunk by themselves.

White wine is one of the best aperitifs—light enough to just whet the appetite for the meal to follow—especially the crisp, bone-dry whites.

White wines are refreshing; they're pleasant and easy to drink. A fresh, young, fruity Chenin Blanc or a youthful Mosel offers the imbiber an engaging charm that is quite delightful.

All of which are reasons enough to believe that the "white wine boom" is not a temporary trend, but that white wine has found its niche in American life. As Americans consume more wine, red wine will also gain in popularity. Wine drinkers will prefer it with certain dishes and not mind in the least the extra efforts. It will complement, but not replace white wine. There are still so many cases where a white wine is just the perfect beverage.

White Wines
—Some Basics

The first difference between white wines and red wines is in the way they begin life. The grapes for red wine are crushed; for white wine, the grapes are pressed.

As practically all wine grapes give white juice—red juice being very rare—the color of a red wine comes, almost always, from the grape skins. Therefore, it is essential to leave the juice in contact with the skins after crushing to make a red wine red. The juice ferments with the skins for a few days to a few weeks, depending on the particular wine and the strength of color desired.

More often than not the grapes are later pressed, but it is this initial step—the crushing—that explains the difference between the white and the red.

Besides extracting color, red wines also extract tannin from the grape skins. Generally, the longer the skin contact, the more tannic the wine. Consequently, red wines can be rough and unready when young.

White wines may be made from white grapes or red grapes (with white juice). In either case, it is desirable to separate the juice from the skins as soon as the grapes are pressed. The juice then ferments alone. Since white wine derives its color from the grape juice rather than the skins, there is no need for skin contact.

And, since the white wines haven't extracted the harsh tannins from the skins, once they are finished fermenting they can be drunk and enjoyed.

Red wines, because they are more complex in their structure and contain tannin, generally need time to become ready to drink. Tannin acts as a preservative. It enables red wines—providing they have the proper balance—to age and develop complexity in the bottle. As the wine matures, the tannins soften and the wine becomes smooth and mellow.

White wines are born drinkable; some whites—in fact most—are best straight from "cask." Bottle age only hurts them. The young wines have a fresh fruitiness that fades with age. For many wines, once the youthful freshness is lost so is the charm. Wines low in acid fade the fastest. Fruit acidity is very important in a wine. The acid helps to preserve the fruit as well as to give life to the wine.

The best white Burgundies and California Chardonnays do improve with age. They develop complexities from maturing in cask (where they pick up tannin from the oak which will allow them to age) and from aging in bottle. But they, too, can be drunk and enjoyed while they are young and fresh, before any cask or bottle aging.

The lusciously sweet wines also age well in the bottle and develop complexities, though they can be enjoyed when young too. In these wines the high sugar level, with sufficient acid, enables them to improve with age.

White wines range in sweetness from the bone-dry Chablis to the lusciously sweet Trockenbeerenauslesen; in body from the delicate Ruwers to the very full, syrupy Sauternes; and in color from the practically colorless young Mosels to the deep amber, almost orange, Trockenbeerenauslesen of the Rheingau.

Generally the young wines are lighter than the mature wines, and the dry wines paler than the sweet wines. The wines from hotter regions tend to be more yellow than those from cooler climes.

The wines, obviously, also range in quality.

The tremendous variety among white wines is created by a number of factors which affect the wines' style and quality. These factors fall into five basic categories: (1) grape variety, (2) soil, (3) climate and weather, (4) vineyard practices, and (5) vinification and cellar treatment.

Among the wine producing grape varieties there are a few, very few, that are capable of producing excellent wines. These are referred to as noble varieties. Among the white wines, Chardonnay and Riesling are truly noble grapes. These varieties are capable of producing wines that have distinctive personalities and improve with age—developing subtle nuances of bouquet and flavor.

There are other grape varieties also capable of producing distinctive wines, varieties such as Gewürztraminer and Pinot Gris. These can be fine wines, but at their best they don't reach the superb heights of the noble varieties.

The majority of grape varieties produce common wines—*vin ordinaire*. They can be pleasant drinking, but that's about all. These are not wines to contemplate or to discuss or even to pay undue attention to. But neither are they to be scorned. They have their place and fill it well enough. And these are often the little wines that travelers in Europe come home with fond memories of, memories which prompt them to search all over town to find a bottle—with disappointing results either way.

Below this are the grape varieties that would be best consumed as table grapes—such as the native American varieties. These grapes are not capable of producing wine at all without considerable human assistance, such as the addition of large quantities of water and sugar.

Another crucial factor in the making of a wine is the soil in the vineyard. In general the best wines come from vineyards planted in what would for most crops be considered poor soil—thin, rocky, dry. The roots have to dig deep for moisture and nutrients. And when they do, they create a more constant environment for the vine, able to better withstand the vagaries of the weather.

It is well known that two vineyards side by side planted with the same grape variety and with all other factors equal, except for the soil, will produce different wines.

Certain types of soil seem ideally suited to certain grape varieties. The chalk in the vineyards of Champagne, for example, seems to be particularly well suited to the Chardonnay grape. On the Mosel, the slate soil of the vineyards is an excellent match for the Riesling vine. The soil contributes to the character of these wines.

The vine is a child of nature, and the climate where the grapes are grown has a very big influence on the wines that are produced. Hot climates tend to produce big wines, high in alcohol and low in acid, with little aroma—robust wines that are generally forthright and dull. The whites from South America and southern Europe are examples. The cooler climes in general produce pale-colored wines, low in alcohol, high in acid, with a more perfumed aroma—delicate wines with subtleties of aroma and flavor. The wines of Germany are a good example of these.

Along with the general climatic conditions, seasonal weather conditions also play a major role. This accounts for the wide variations which can be found from vintage to vintage in wine from the same vineyard.

Of all the factors affecting quality, weather is the most variable, especially in the more northerly regions such as Germany and parts of France and California. Weather, although still a factor, is less so in the sunny southern areas of Spain, France, Italy, Portugal, and California.

In certain favored years in Germany, France, Hungary, and the United States, the conditions are just right to produce the Botrytis cinerea mold on the grapes, which makes possible the lusciously sweet dessert wines such as the Sauternes and the Auslesen. In other years there may be too much rain and not enough sun. Then some of the northern wines can only be made by chaptalisation—adding sugar to the must, the natural grape sugar being insufficient to produce the necessary alcohol.

Generally the cooler northern climates produce the best white wines. Here the grapes ripen more slowly, developing subtleties of aroma and flavor. And the wines are well-balanced with refreshing acidity.

Another important factor affecting the style and quality of a wine is vineyard practice. How the vines are trained, how well they are pruned, whether they are irrigated, if the crop is thinned—these and many other vineyard practices all have an effect on the wine that will be produced.

Too large a crop will result in lighter, less flavorful wines; smaller crops, in more concentration of fruit and flavor.

Irrigating too much or too close to harvest will water down the wine.

The final determining factors in what type of wine will be produced are vinification and cellar treatment.

Long fermentation at low temperatures—a widespread practice in Germany and California—helps to preserve the freshness and natural fruitiness of white wine.

The handling of the wine during vinification also determines its style. Dry wines are wines that have completely fermented; that is, all of their sugar has been converted into alcohol. In making an off-dry or semi-sweet wine, either the fermentation is stopped while some of the sugar remains, or a sweetener— such as unfermented grape juice or a sweet concentrated wine—is added after fermentation has run its course. There are many methods. The grapes—or should we say raisins—for the lusciously sweet wines and the Passitos contain so much sugar that an alcohol level high enough to stop fermentation is reached while there is still a high concentration of sweetness in the wine.

Stainless steel or glass-lined concrete tanks for storage and holding help to preserve the freshness and flavor of the white wines. Oak casks add to the character of some wines— Chardonnay, for example. But for others, the use of wooden casks detracts from the wine's character, resulting in a dull, oxidized wine. Many of the wines from eastern Europe, southern Europe, and South America fall into this category. But these wines have been much improved where the practice of using cool fermentation and stainless steel or glass-lined storage tanks has been adopted.

White wine when young can be charming and refreshing; mature white wine can be fine and complex. The dry whites are an excellent accompaniment to meals, and the lusciously sweet whites are excellent with fruit or sipped by themselves.

White wines may be classified by taste into six categories: bone-dry, dry, off-dry, semi-sweet, sweet, and lusciously sweet.

Bone Dry

The bone-dry wines are pale in color, with sometimes a slight greenish hue. These are the driest of the dry wines. They have higher acidity than the wines classified simply as dry. In these wines dryness is really their essence. They are crisp and have a cleansing effect in the mouth.

The best example of a bone-dry wine is Chablis—the true Chablis from France, of course. Other examples are Muscadet, Sancerre, Pouilly Fumé, and Coteaux Champenois.

Because of their acidity and uncompromising dryness, these wines are better drunk with food than without. They go very well with shellfish and the more definitely flavored salt-water fish. In fact, they have a similar effect to the lemon served with these seafood dishes in sparking their flavor.

Dry

The next step up on the scale are the dry wines. These wines may be actually as dry as the bone-dry wines, but they don't feel as dry on the palate. They are balanced by a fruitiness which makes them less austere.

Some examples of the dry wines: white Burgundies from the Côte d'Or and Mâcon, Alsatian Riesling, New York Chardonnay and Riesling, California Chardonnay and Sauvignon Blanc, Sylvaner from Franconia, Austrian Sylvaner and Riesling, Swiss Fendant, Soave, Verdicchio, Franciacorta Pinot, and Blanc de Morgex from Italy.

These wines make a fine aperitif; they also go well with

fresh-water fish, the more delicately flavored salt-water fish, poultry, and veal. The bigger wines may also accompany pork.

Off-Dry

The wines described as off-dry have a hint of sweetness—just enough to soften the wine. They are often lower in acid than the dry wines—taking two wines from the same region and same variety, in general the drier the wine, the higher the acid.

The off-dry wines include German Riesling Kabinett and most Spätlesen, some California Riesling and Chenin Blanc, Frascati, and Condrieu.

The off-dry wines are a good accompaniment to seafood or fresh-water fish simply prepared or in a cream sauce, pasta in cream sauce, poultry and veal broiled, sauteed, or prepared with a hint of sweetness such as with cream or fruit sauces.

Semi-Sweet

The semi-sweet wines have a noticeable sweetness, but are not fully sweet. Examples of semi-sweet wines: many California Chenin Blancs, German Auslesen and the sweeter Spätlesen, and Italian Amabile and Abboccato wines.

These wines are perhaps best drunk alone, but may accompany poultry or veal in sweet or cream sauces.

Sweet

The sweet wines are golden and fully sweet, with high sugar levels. Examples of sweet wines are Sauternes, Barsac, Quarts de Chaume, Bonnezeaux, some California Chenin Blancs and Sémillons, German Auslesen, and the Italian Passito wines.

These wines go well with some desserts—ripe fruit, tartes or cakes if not too sweet, such as pound cake. But they may also be the dessert, simply sipped by themselves.

Lusciously Sweet

The lusciously sweet wines are deeply golden. They may not be sweeter, but are richer than the sweet wines. These wines generally have been intensified by noble rot on the grapes which adds depth of character and complexity to the wines.

Among the lusciously sweet wines are the Beerenauslesen, Trockenbeerenauslesen, Tokaji Aszu, the more intense Sauternes and Barsacs, and the richer Quarts de Chaume, Vouvray, and Bonnezeaux.

These wines are excellent sipped alone (and contemplated). They may also accompany stoned fruits such as nectarines, peaches, or plums. And surprisingly they also go with the marbled cheeses such as Roquefort and Gorgonzola.

How to Use this Guide

The aim of this guide is to provide information on the white wines of the world, a very large and varied collection. It is written for all those who drink and enjoy white wine and also for those who think they might like to try it. The guide is intended to be as informative and valuable to the wine drinker as possible—in pointing out what to expect from unfamiliar wines, areas, or producers, as well as adding to the reader's knowledge of the more familiar wines.

Many of the wines listed are very well known, others less so. Some which are listed are not currently available in many parts of the United States. But these are wines that can be expected to be imported or to become more widely available in the future. And, of course, these entries like the others will be useful to the traveler tasting the wines in their country of origin.

The major part of the guide is the dictionary section, providing information on wine-producing countries, major wine regions, districts, and towns, common label terms, grape varieties, and wine names—geographical, varietal, proprietary, generic, and fantasy names. American producers are also listed, as in the United States it is more meaningful to discuss individual wineries than it is wine towns. In fact, a town name seldom appears on an American label.

So, the best white wines of an American winery are listed under the producer's name, while the better European producers and vineyards are listed under town names. Where a particular producer has been omitted, though, it is not necessarily the case that his wines are not recommended.

All entries are followed by a country code except for names of countries, grape varieties (which cross borders), and generic names (which may be used—or misused—in more than one country).

As.—Australia
Au.—Austria
Bl.—Bulgaria
Cy.—Cyprus
Cz.—Czechoslovakia
Fr.—France
Gm.—Germany
Gc.—Greece
Hn.—Hungary
It.—Italy
Pr.—Portugal
Rm.—Rumania
S.A.—South Africa
Sp.—Spain
Sw.—Switzerland
U.S.—United States
Yg.—Yugoslavia

The wine laws of France, Italy and Germany are explained to clarify the mysteries of AC, DOC, Q.b.A, etc.; and where pitfalls exist in those laws, these are pointed out.

The wines are described and evaluated according to their

relative value in the marketplace. The wines are judged not only for quality but also for value.

Note is also made of certain wines which must be drunk young to be best appreciated, especially in cases where they are not often seen in this country until they are already old and tired. This reflects personal tastes, of course, but the tastes of knowledgeable wine drinkers in general have been taken into consideration.

Personal tastes are also a factor in matching wine with food, though there are certain practical guidelines which do apply. If either the food or the wine overpowers the flavor of the other, for example, they are not well matched.

But the suggestions, at any rate, are just that; there is no right or wrong in matters of taste. Or, if there is, it is only that it is wrong to say that you should or shouldn't like a particular thing—in this case, wine or combination. In the final analysis, the decision is between the taster and his (her) palate.

To find information on a particular wine, the first place to look is under the wine name (often, though not always, the most prominent name on the label). If that does not prove successful, or does not answer all your questions, try next in the cross reference under the country of origin matching the terms on the label with the names in the listing and then checking those entries.

The cross reference index lists, by country, all entries in the dictionary section for that country to facilitate fact finding and to make tracking down a particular wine, grape variety, etc., that much easier.

Dictionary A–Z

Abymes, Fr. A dry, light to medium-bodied wine from the Haute-Savoie in southeastern France.

Abboccato, It. Semi-sweet.

Abocado, Sp. Semi-sweet.

Abymes, Fr. A dry, light to medium-bodied wine from the Haute-Savoie in southeastern France.

AC see France.

Agros, Cy. A sweet dessert wine made from Muscat grapes on Cyprus.

Aguamurcia, Sp. A dry to semi-sweet white wine from Catalonia in northeastern Spain.

Aguilar de la Frontera, Sp. A full and robust white wine with high alcohol from southern Spain.

Ahr, Gm. One of the eleven wine-producing regions (Anbaugebiete) of Germany; the second smallest. The Ahr is in the northwestern part of Germany's grape-growing area. Production here is almost evenly divided between red and white wines. This region is actually better known for its red wines, but some quite respectable light, off-dry, white wines are also produced. Riesling and Müller-Thurgau are the major white grape varieties. The Bereich (subregion) is Walporzheim/Ahrtal; the Grosslage (general site), Klosterberg.

Aigle, Sw.   One of the better wine towns of the Chablais (see) in the Vaud canton east of Geneva, producing light, dry whites from the Fendant grape (see).

Albalonga   One of the new German hybrid grapes; a cross between Sylvaner and hybrid Rieslaner producing light, fruity wines with some charm and style.

Albana di Romagna, It.   A full-bodied white wine ranging from dry to semi-sweet. It's made from the Albana grape grown in Emilia–Romagna in central Italy. The dry version goes well with seafood; the semi-sweet, with poultry or veal in cream sauces. This wine generally ranges in quality from ordinary to fair; some good bottles are produced. Notable producers: Giuseppe Marabini, Pasolini, Mario Pezzi.

Albania   This Balkan country produces ordinary to fair white wines. Few Albanian whites of consequence are seen in the United States.

Albano, It.   A dry, pleasant quaffing wine from the Alban hills outside of Rome. This wine can be a good thirst-quencher when consumed young, while it maintains its youthful freshness. (See Castelli Romani.)

Alcamo or **Bianco Alcamo, It.**   A greenish straw, full-bodied, heavy Sicilian wine. It is generally lacking in acid, but is suitable for drinking with highly spiced seafood or poultry dishes. Serve well-chilled.

Alcobaca, Pr.   A good-quality white wine from coastal vineyards in Portugal.

Alella, Sp.   A white wine from the town of the same name in

Catalonia north of Barcelona. This wine ranges from off-dry to semi-sweet.

Algeria This North African country produces very little white wine of consequence. Most is heavy and coarse, low in acidity, and high in alcohol. Some fair-quality whites are produced in the Coteau de Mascara.

Aligoté This grape produces some undistinguished, but pleasant, white Burgundies, usually labeled Bourgogne Aligoté. They are best consumed within a year or two of the vintage, and can be a pleasant accompaniment to poultry and fish dishes, especially those with oily sauces (because of the wine's relatively high acidity), or pork, and they go particularly well with Escargots (snails) à la Bourguignonne. Dr. Konstantin Frank (see) produces small quantities of Aligoté in his New York State vineyard which, thus far at least, have been low in fruit and high in acid.

Almadén, U.S. A California winery that produces a respectable, moderately priced Gewürztraminer (see).

Aloxe-Corton, Fr. The northernmost wine village of importance in the Côte de Beaune district of Burgundy, unusual in that it is highly regarded for both its reds and whites. The white wines generally come from the vineyards on the upper hillsides. The lesser wines are sold under the Aloxe-Corton name; the better ones carry the name of the vineyard. Some of the wines from Ladoix-Serrigny and Pernand-Vergelesses, two adjoining villages, are also entitled to be sold under the Aloxe-Corton name. Aloxe-Corton has three grand crus: Corton, Charlemagne, and Corton-Charlemagne (see under individual listings). The whites of Aloxe-Corton are dry, full-flavored, and with a firm texture but an underlying softness that causes some tasters to compare them to the wines of Meursault (see). These wines go well with salt-water fish such as bass and flounder, and delicate meat such as roast veal or white-meat chicken.

Alsace, Fr. A wine-producing region in northeastern France lying between the Vosges Mountains and the Rhine. The vineyards are on the hillsides flanking a pictur-esque region dotted with medieval villages of half-timbered houses with bright flower boxes and an occasional stork's nest on the chimney. The 30,000 acres of vines, held by approximately 50,000 proprie-tors, produce some 17 million gallons of wine annually. Most of it is white, dry, fresh, and crisp, with a lively fruit acidity and a touch of spiciness. These wines, in the slender flute bottles, are usually named for their grape variety. The same varieties are grown here as in Germany, but unlike their German cousins, the Alsa-tian wines are at their best with food. They go well with rich, creamy dishes and are fitting accompani-ment to pork and goose (as in the local cuisine). Alsatian wines achieving 11% or more of natural alcohol can be labeled Grand Vin, Grand Cru, Réserve Speciale, Grande Réserve, or Réserve Exceptionelle. These wines, too, are usually dry, but sometimes they are off-dry and occasionally semi-sweet. Wines labeled Vendange Tardive, made from late-picked grapes, usually range from off-dry to semi-sweet.

The noble *Riesling* is the undisputed king of Alsatian wines. This wine has a full, but delicate aroma, is dry and crisp, medium- to full-bodied and with more power and authority than the German Rieslings. Some fine Rieslings come from Riquewihr Kellenberg and Ribeauvillé Dambach. They are good as an aperitif, or with shellfish such as scallops or shrimp, and also go well with poultry and veal.

Gewürztraminer is next in esteem, and indeed almost no place on earth produces Gewürztraminers of such high quality. These wines have a distinctive spicy bouquet. They are usually dry, crisp, fruity, and full, with refreshing acidity, and a lingering spiciness. Gewürztraminer goes well with foie gras (a local specialty) and spicy poultry, veal, lamb, or fish dishes. Try it with curry.

Traminer, rarely seen nowadays, is similar to Gewürztraminer but with a less pronounced spiciness.

Muscat d'Alsace is dry and fruity with medium body and full flavor. It has a pronounced fruity-spicy (Muscat) aroma, and makes a good aperitif.

Tokay d'Alsace, the local name for the Pinot Gris, is generally dry but some off-dry is also made. This wine will live for many years while retaining its freshness. It is generally full-bodied and balanced with pleasing acidity. It goes as well with poultry or veal as with fresh-water fish.

Pinot Blanc is one variety which is not very successful in Alsace, producing wines that tend to be rather neutral.

Sylvaner is fruitier, lighter in body, and with less distinction than the Riesling. It has a slight but pleasant fruity aroma. Sylvaner goes well with fresh- or salt-water fish, veal, or poultry.

A blend of any of the above varieties, and only those varieties, can be labeled *Edelzwicker* (noble blend).

Other varieties grown in Alsace producing rather ordinary, neutral wines which can be pleasant to drink with fish and poultry: Auxerrois Blanc, Chasselas, and Knipperlé.

Some of the highly regarded shipper-producers: Leon Beyer (especially outstanding Gewürztraminer), Dopff, Dopff et Irion, Hugel (some very fine Riesling and quite a good Tokay d'Alsace), Preisszimmer, Schlumberger, Trimbach, and Willm (a very fine Gewürztraminer from their Clos Gaensbroennel vineyard).

Alto Adige, It. The northernmost province of Italy, producing some of Italy's best white wines. They are best drunk as young as possible, while they still retain their youthful freshness and charm. The controlled denomination of origin (DOC), Alto Adige or Süd Tyrol, comprises 33 villages in the province of Bolzano. The climate here is alpine, but the surrounding mountains act as a barrier to the cold winds from the north. The wines of this bilingual region are named for their predominant grape variety.

Moscato Giallo, or *Goldenmuskateller,* is an aromatic wine with a pleasant sweetish flavor. It makes a good aperitif or pleasant sipping wine.

Pinot Grigio, or *Ruländer,* is a dry, crisp, and fruity wine. It goes well with shellfish, and delicate salt-water fish.

Pinot Bianco, or *Weissburgunder,* has a vinous aroma. It is light to medium in body, dry, crisp, and fruity, but has less distinction than the Pinot Grigio.

The *Riesling Renano,* or *Rheinriesling,* produces a more distinguished wine than the *Riesling Italico,* or

Welschriesling. Both wines are straw-colored with a greenish tint. They have a vinous aroma and a dry, fresh, fruity flavor.

Quite similar to these are the *Sylvaner* and the *Riesling X Sylvaner,* or *Müller–Thurgau.* These two wines are somewhat more delicate than the above-mentioned Rieslings. All four go well with fresh-water fish, chicken, and veal.

Sauvignon, with a greenish tint, is dry and fruity with refreshing acidity. It goes well with lightly spiced seafood and poultry.

Traminer Aromatico, or *Gewürztraminer,* is golden in color, aromatic, and has a full and fruity flavor. This wine stands up to spicy fish, veal, and poultry dishes.

All of these wines should be consumed as young as possible.

Herrnhofer, Joseph Hofstatter, and Schloss Kehlburg are respected producers, as are the Abbazia di Novacella, Convento dei Benedettini di Muri, and the Cantina Sociale di Termeno. (See also Terlano, Valdadige, Valle Isarco.)

Amabile, It. Semi-sweet.

Amboise See Touraine Amboise.

Amigne See Valais.

Ammerschwihr, Fr. An Alsatian village known for its Rieslings and Gewürztraminers. Its best vineyard: Kaeferkopf.

Anjou, Fr. A region in western central France encompassing both sides of the Loire River and some of its tributaries. Sixty pe cent of the wines from Anjou are white. Even the lesser of them can be, and often are, quite charming. They are from the Chenin Blanc, the only white grape of consequence grown here. These wines range from off-dry to lusciously sweet, and the better the wine, the sweeter it is. The more common wines are labeled Anjou Blanc or Chenin d'Anjou. The better ones have more specific geographical information on the label.

The Coteaux de la Loire (see) and Coteaux du Layon (see) are the most important areas. (See also Coteaux de l'Aubance, Coteaux du Loir, and Saumur.)

The drier Anjous go well with poultry, the sweeter ones with fruit; the in-betweens make pleasant sipping beverages on hot summer afternoons.

Annecy, Fr.   A district in the Haute-Savoie producing some agreeable white wines that make fine accompaniment to fresh-water fish and fowl.

Aquileia, It.   A controlled denomination of origin (DOC) in Friuli-Venezia-Giulia (see) in northeastern Italy. These wines are labeled for their grape variety.

Tocai Friulano is pale straw in color, with a delicate vinous aroma. It is medium-bodied and dry.

Pinot Bianco is a rather soft, neutral wine with little distinction.

Pinot Grigio is full-bodied and dry, and at its best rather crisp.

Riesling Renano, ranging from medium- to full-bodied, is a dry wine that can be pleasantly fruity.

These wines, like most Italian whites, are best consumed as young as possible as they are generally low in acid.

Arbalète, Clos de l', Sw.   A noted vineyard in Dézaley (see Vaud).

Arbois, Fr.   The best-known wine-producing area of the Jura (see) in eastern France. These wines are made from the Savagnin grape. They go well with richly flavored fish, poultry or veal dishes. Some of the more noted wines of Arbois are Vin Jaune (see) and Vin de Paille (see Paille, Vin de).

Arche, Château d', Fr.　A second-growth Sauternes (see).

Argentina　Argentina has the biggest wine production of any country in the western hemisphere. The most important wine-producing area is the province of Mendoza in the foothills of the Andes. The white grape varieties grown in Argentina include Riesling, Pinot Blanc, Chardonnay, Chenin Blanc, Sémillon, and Sauvignon.

Most of the white wine lacks distinction. It tends to be rather bland and ordinary, with an oxidized flavor from too long wood aging. There seems to be a growing awareness, though, of technological improvements, such as cold fermentation and stainless steel tanks. So Argentina might be a country to watch for its white wines.

Arlot, Clos de l', Fr.　A premier cru wine of Prémeaux, usually sold under the Nuits-St.-Georges (see) appellation. It is one of the few white wines produced in the Côte de Nuits (see) section of Burgundy (see). Jules Belin is a good producer.

Arubti　A grape variety grown in the Dão, Bucellas (see), and Colares regions of Portugal. The wines can be pleasant accompaniment to seafood such as shellfish or oily fish appetizers.

Aszu　See Tokaji.

Aubance, Coteaux de l'　See Coteaux de l'Aubance.

Aurora Blanc　A French-American hybrid grape variety producing soft, fragrant wines, usually without much distinction. Bully Hill Winery, of New York State, produces a respectable Aurora Blanc.

Auslese, Gm. Specially selected bunches of late-ripened grapes, often but not always affected by Edelfäule, or "noble rot" (see Botrytis cinerea). The wines made from these grapes range from semi-sweet to sweet. Generally best as sipping wines, unaccompanied by food, they do go well with peaches and nectarines. Auslese is one of the predicates allowed under the new German wine laws (1971) on German wines labeled Qualitätswein mit Prädikat (see).

Auslesen, Gm. This term is used to refer to the class of wines including Auslese (see), Beerenauslese (see) and Trockenbeerenauslese (see).

Australia Australia produces a wide range of white wines. Most are pleasant and mellow, but soft, being low in acidity. They are best served well-chilled, with food. Like California wines, they are named for European wine regions (Chablis, Burgundy, etc.) or with a grape name, sometimes with a regional qualifier. Technology has done a lot to improve these wines. By fermenting in stainless steel tanks the temperature can be kept low to help preserve the freshness and fruitiness of the wines.

Among the grape varieties grown for white wine is Riesling, generally Australia's best white. As often as not, though, a wine labeled Riesling will be from the Sémillon grape. The name Riesling apparently means only white wine here. True Rieslings are generally labeled Rhine Riesling. These wines can be pleasant enough although generally lacking the balance of their German and Alsatian counterparts; they are more in the style of the California Rieslings. These wines go well with veal or poultry in cream sauces. The best Rhine Rieslings come from Coonawarra and the Barossa Valley (see). Some good ones bear the labels of Kaiserstuhl (see), Gramp's Steingarten, Penfold's Eden Valley, and Yalumba's Pewsey Vale.

Other white grapes grown in Australia are Blanquette, Chardonnay (very little), Chasselas, Marsanne, Palomino, Sauvignon Blanc, Sémillon, Traminer, and Verdelho. These wines are generally undistinguished.

Of Australia's major wine-producing regions, South Australia is responsible for about two-thirds of the viticultural output. Its major wine areas are Coonawarra, Clare, Hope Valley, Kefefroch, Langhorne Creek, Modbury, Murray River Valley, and Watervale. Light wines are produced at both Clare and Watervale.

New South Wales is next in terms of quantity, with wines from Corowa, Hunter River Valley (see), and the Murrumbidgee flats.

Wines are also produced in the Barossa Valley (see), Magill, McLaren Vale, and Swan Valley in Western Australia.

In Victoria, vines grow in Avoca, Glenrowan, Great Western, Mildura, Rutherglen, Tahbilk, and Wangaratta.

The smallest wine-producing province is Queensland, with wines made at Fordes, Mudgee, and Rooty Hill.

Austria The white wines of Austria, like those of the Italian Tyrol (Alto Adige) and Alsace, are generally made from the same grapes as the German wines, but unlike the Germans, they produce wines that are best with food rather than as sipping beverages. These wines, for the most part, are best when very young, while they retain a certain freshness and charm.

As in Germany also, in better years, Austria produces wines ranging from off-dry to lusciously sweet, labeled Spätlese, Auslese, Beerenauslese, and Trockenbeeren-auslese (see individual listings) depending on the degree of sweetness and the condition of the grapes. These wines may be best appreciated when sipped without food, though the sweeter ones can accompany ripe fruit.

In general, Austrian wines are low in alcohol (though not as low as the German wines), dry and fruity, and with refreshing acidity. These wines go well with shellfish, such as scallops, clams, or shrimp, and fresh- or salt-water fish, or simply cooked chicken and veal dishes (wienerschnitzel). Because of their lightness they also make a fine aperitif.

Austrian wines are generally named for the region and grape variety they are from. The wine-producing regions are Lower Austria (Niederösterreich), Burgenland, Styria (Steiermark), and Vienna (Wien).

Lower Austria produces nearly two-thirds of all Austrian wine. This region is subdivided into Baden, Donauland, Krems, Langenlois, Vöslau, Wachau, and Wienviertel.

Baden produces Austria's most noted wine, Gumpolds-kirchner (see). Wines are also produced at Pfaff-stätten and Traiskirchen from Neuburger and Zierfandler grapes.

Wines in Donauland are produced at Kloster-

neuberg, Leithagebirge, Prellenkirchen, and Trais-
mauer from Grüner Veltliner, Rhine Riesling, Müller-
Thurgau, Pinot Blanc, and Traminer grapes. Grüner
Veltliner, Rhine Riesling, Neuburger, and Müller-
Thurgau varieties are grown in Langenlois at Schön-
berg, Strass, and Zöbing.

Very little white wine is produced in Vöslau.

Burgenland, subdivided into Eisenberg, Neusiedlersee, and Rust (see), is responsible for nearly one-
third of all Austrian wines, most of which are red.
Some good dessert wines are made here also. Wines
from Rust, labeled Ruster Ausbruch, are made from
overripe Muscat Ottonel and Furmint grapes and are
richly sweet. These wines go well with fruit. Some
good wine towns in Rust include Breitenbrunn, Don-
nerkirchen, Eisenstadt, Gross-Höflein, Jois, Klein-
Höflein, Mattersburg, Mörbisch (famous for its Muscats), Neusiedl, Oggau, Pöttelsdorf, Purbach, St. Georgen, St. Margarethen, and Widen. Wines are produced
from the Wälschriesling, Neuburger, Pinot Blanc or
Weisser Burgunder, Traminer, and Grüner Veltliner
grape varieties.

Neusiedlersee wines are made at Gols, Halnturn,
Mönchhof, Seewinkel, and Weiden from the Wälsch-
riesling, Neuburger, Pinot Blanc, Muscat Ottonel, and
Traminer grapes.

Little white wine of consequence is produced at
Eisenberg.

Southern Styria (Südsteiermark) grows Wälschriesling, Sauvignon, Klevner (Pinot Blanc), Muskat X
Sylvaner, Yellow Muskateller, Gewürztraminer, and

Morillon at Ehrenhausen, Glanz, Kitzek, Leibnitz, Leutschach, Ottenberg, Ratsch, Schlossberg, Sousal, Spielfeld, and Sutztal.

In the Klöch-East Styria (Klöch-Oststeiermark) area, wines are produced at Hartberg, Klöch, Mureck, and Radkersburg, from the Traminer, Wälschriesling, Pinot Gris, Rhine Riesling, and Muskat X Sylvaner varieties.

In western Styria (Weststeiermark) a little white wine is produced from Müller-Thurgau and Wälschriesling grown at Deutschlandberg, Graz, St. Stefan, Ost, and Stainz.

Grüner Veltliner, Traminer, Sylvaner, and both Rhine Riesling and Wälschriesling are grown in the suburbs of Vienna at Grinzing, in Heiligenstadt, Nussberg, and Perchtoldsdorf.

Austrian wines today represent outstanding value, perhaps because they are still little known. Some very fine values can be found, which will make good drinking with fish, poultry, pork, and veal dishes.

Auxerrois A clone of the Pinot Blanc (see) variety grown in Luxembourg, France—in Lorraine, and Germany—in Baden and the Palatinate (Rheinpfalz).

Auxey-Duresses, Fr. A wine village in the Côte de Beaune (see) district of Burgundy. While not so fine as Meursault, which they have an affinity to, some good wines of excellent value are produced here. These little-known wines apparently lack popularity because of their name, which Americans seem to find difficult to pronounce. The white Auxey-Duresses is a good wine with veal and chicken dishes. Reliable producers: Louis Latour, Leroy.

Avelsbach(er), Gm. The wines of Avelsbach, a wine town on the Mosel, are now, under the new German wine laws, sold as Trierer wines. Avelsbacher vineyards: Altenberg, Domherrenberg, Hammerstein, Herrenberg, Kupp, and Rotlay. Reliable producers: Bischhöfliches Konvikt, Hohe Domkirche, and Staatlichen Weinbaudomänen. Some Ruländer, unusual in the Mosel, is planted.

Ayl(er), Gm. Ayl is one of the better wine towns on the Saar (see). Ayler vineyards: Herrenberger, Kupp, and Scheidterberger. Reliable producers include Bischhöfliches Konvikt, Bischhöfliches Priesterseminar, Thiergarten Georg Fritz von Nell.

Azay-le-Rideau, Fr. This town in Touraine produces some pleasant, fruity white wines from the Chenin Blanc grape, ranging from off-dry to semi-sweet (see Touraine; Chenin Blanc).

Azeitão, Pr. A bone-dry, crisp, fruity Portuguese white wine.

Bacchus A new German hybrid, a cross of Sylvaner with Riesling and Müller-Thurgau, named no doubt for the god of wine.

Bad Dürkheim See Dürkheim.

Bad Kreuznach See Kreuznach.

Badacsony, Hn. A wine-producing area in Hungary named for an extinct volcano and known for its white wines. They are usually named for the grape variety and labeled Badacsonyi followed by the grape name. These wines are generally sweeter, stronger, and more aromatic than those of the Balaton area (see). These wines go with spicy seafood and poultry dishes.

Badacsonyi Furmint is a full-bodied white wine with some sugar.

Badacsonyi Hárslevelü is one of the area's leading white wines, from the Hárslevelü grape.

Badacsonyi Kéknyelü is a dry to semi-sweet wine. The drier version is more often seen in the United States. Reputedly one of the best wines of Hungary.

Badacsonyi Muskotaly is made from the Muscatel grape.

Badacsonyi Rizling, from the Riesling grape (see), is generally regarded as the best white wine of the region.

Badacsonyi Szürkebarát (literally, "gray friar"), from the Pinot Gris, is off-dry, mellow, and quite full-bodied.

Badacsonyi See Badacsony.

Baden, Au. A village in lower Austria producing some quite acceptable white wines. (See Austria.)

Baden, Gm. One of Germany's eleven wine regions (Anbaugebiete), stretching from Lake Constance (Bodensee) to the Badische Bergstrasse in southwestern Germany. The Baden wines, like those of Franconia and Württemberg, are more like the wines of Austria and Alsace than those of the Mosel and Rhine in that they go well with food, and are drier and fuller in body than the Rhines and Mosels. The major white grape varieties of Baden are Müller-Thurgau, Ruländer, Gutedel, Riesling, and Sylvaner. Weissburgunder, Gewürztraminer, and Traminer are also planted. Over three-fourths of the Baden wines are white. Baden is subdivided into seven subregions (Bereich): Badische Bergstrasse/Kraichgau, Badisches Frankenland, Bodensee, Breisgau, Kaiserstuhl-Tuniberg, Markgräflerland, and Ortenau. The wines from the Badisches Frankenland, like those of Franconia, are bottled in a short, wide-bellied Bocksbeutel.

Badische Bergstrasse/Kraichgau produces Rieslings and Ruländers. The Ruländers can be quite good, and are among the best in the world produced from that variety.

Ortenau grows Riesling, Traminer, and Ruländer. The Riesling here is called Klingelberger.

Markgräflerland produces some good Sylvaners and Rieslings, and perhaps the best Traminers of Germany. The Gutedel (see) grape, quite common here, is responsible for some low-acid, pleasant, mild quaffing wines.

Kaiserstuhl-Tuniberg grows Ruländer, Gewürztraminer, Riesling, and Sylvaner. These wines can be heavy, but make a suitable accompaniment to spicy fish dishes.

Breisgau is known for its Weissherbst, a white wine made from red grapes.

The wines from the Bodensee (Lake Constance) are known as Seeweine. These wines, often made from Ruländer or Gewürztraminer grapes, can be somewhat heavy and awkward, but few are exported to this country.

Some 80% of the Baden wines are produced by 120 cooperatives, with 23,000 members. Baden wines are known for their freshness and fullness. They are better with food—fresh-water fish, poultry, veal in sauce—than alone as sipping wines. Schloss Neumeier in Mauerberg is one of the better Baden wines seen in the United States.

Bairrada, Pr. A full-bodied white wine from Portugal.

Balaton, Hn. A wine-producing region of Hungary on the shores of Lake Balaton, the largest lake in Europe. This region is noted for its Rizling (Riesling) and Furmint. These wines are generally labeled Balatoni followed by the grape name.

Balatoni See Balaton.

Bandol, Fr. This region in southern France produces some pleasant white wines—better than ordinary—from the Clairette and Ugni Blanc grapes. They are a good beverage to accompany seafood dishes, particularly those in piquant or spicy sauces.

Banyuls, Fr. A well-known fortified dessert wine made from the Grenache grape.

Baret, Château, Fr. This Bordeaux château produces some good white Graves (see).

Barossa Valley, As. The origin of some of Australia's best whites, especially those from the Rhine Riesling, something of a specialty. The Barossa Valley Cooperative produces some good wines under the Kaiserstuhl (see) label. Other regarded producers: Gramp's Orlando, Hamilton's Springton, Henschke's Keyneton, and Yalumba.

Barsac, Fr. One of the five communes of Sauternes, and the only one entitled to use either the name of the village, Barsac, or of Sauternes. These wines are generally less sweet than those of the other Sauternes villages, though they are quite sweet. The Barsacs are known for their delicacy and breed. The overall quality of Barsac can be seen by the fact that nine of the twenty-four classified growths of Sauternes—Châteaux Broustet, Caillou, Climens, Coutet, Doisey-Daëne, Doisey-Védrines, de Myrat, Nairac, and Suau—are from Barsac.

Bâtard-Montrachet, Fr. One of the greatest dry white wine vineyards in the world, ranked as a grand cru in Burgundy and only one notch below Montrachet itself. The 28-acre Bâtard-Montrachet vineyard is divided between Chassagne and Puligny-Montrachet. This pale golden wine is relatively high in alcohol, dry, and full-flavored with outstanding bouquet and flavor. It is a fine wine to accompany simple veal or poultry dishes. Fine producers: Prosper Maufoux, Max Brenot, Delegrange Bacchelet, Latour, Jadot, Leroy.

Béarn, Fr. This region in southwest France produces some dry, as well as some sweet, white wines. The best known is Jurançon (see). Others also well regarded: Rousselet de Béarn, Vin de Béarn.

Beaujolais, Fr. A region much better known for its light red wines, but which also produces some whites from the Chardonnay grape. They are similar in style to those from Mâcon (see) to the north. Prosper Maufoux makes a good Beaujolais Blanc, as does Louis Jadot.

Beaulieu-sur-Layon See Coteaux du Layon.

Beaulieu Vineyards (BV), U.S. This California vineyard, in Napa Valley, produces good Pinot Chardonnay wines.

Beaumes de Venise, Fr. A fortified dessert or aperitif wine made from Muscat grapes grown in the southern Côtes du Rhône. One of the better French muscats. Drink alone or with nuts.

Beaune, Fr. The major town of the Côte de Beaune (see) to which it gives its name. Most of the wines of Beaune are red. Clos des Mouches, a premier cru, produces mostly red wines but some fine whites as well, notably those of Joseph Drouhin. These wines, like those of Meursault, have an underlying softness. They go well with veal and poultry.

Beerenauslese A lusciously sweet wine made from specially selected overripe grapes. The grapes have quite often been affected by Edelfäule, the "noble mold" (see Botrytis cinerea). These wines are rare and expensive. Even in the better vintages, very little of this wine is made. The labor alone makes it quite expensive. The best Beerenauslesen are from the Riesling grape, and produced in the Mosel-Saar-Ruwer and Rheingau regions of Germany.

Bellegarde, Clairette de See Clairette de Bellegarde.

Bellet, Fr. The wine from this area, near Nice, is mostly rosé, but white wine is sometimes also produced.

Bereich, Gm. A German subregion, comprising several townships and vineyards. The label of a wine named for the Bereich (rather than a vineyard or Grosslage) must use the word Bereich either before or after the subregion name. Within a Bereich the wines of the different vineyards and villages must be similar in taste and bouquet.

Bergerac, Fr. Most of the white wine of Bergerac is of fair quality. The best wines have their own controlled appellations of origin (AC): Monbazillac (see), Montravel (see), and Rosette (see).

Bergheim, Fr. An Alsatian wine town known for its Rieslings and Gewürztraminers. A noted vineyard: Kanzlerberg.

Bergstrasse See Hessische Bergstrasse and Baden (Badische Bergstrasse).

Beringer, U.S. A Napa Valley-based winery which produces a pleasant, mellow white wine labeled Traubengold and an agreeable Fumé Blanc. It also makes a good Malvasia Bianca.

Bernkastel(er), Gm. Bernkastel is perhaps the most famous wine town on the Mosel. It is here that the famous Doktor vineyard is located. The other vineyards in the Badstube Grosslage: Bratenhöfchen, Graben, Lay, and Matheisbildchen. The Bernkasteler wines are known for their delicacy and lightness. They are among the driest of the Mosels. Some tasters claim to detect a stony, minerally taste. Respected producers: Adams Bergweiler, Pauly-Bergweiler, Geller, Kath. Pfarrkirche St. Michael, Liell, Dr. Melsheimer, J. J. Prüm, St. Nikolaus Hospital, Thaprich, and the three owners of Bernkasteler Doktor (or Doctor)—Deinhard, Lauerburg, and Thanisch. Bernkasteler Doktor is without question the most expensive wine of the Mosel. There is some difference of opinion over whether it is the best. Since the new German wine laws (1971) have nearly tripled its size from 3½ to nearly 10 acres, one wonders how long it will continue to fetch such high prices, and to retain its reputation. There is some doubt that stretching the vineyard's name to cover adjoining properties does anything to improve the quality of those vineyards. Deinhard owned 1¾ acres, Thanisch an acre and a half, and Lauerburg one-quarter acre of the original Doktor vineyard. At one time, Dr. Thanisch sold his wine as Bernkasteler Doktor und Graben; Lauerburg, his as Bernkasteler Doktor und Bratenhöfchen; and Deinhard either as Bernkasteler Doktor und Badstube or simply Bernkasteler Doktor.

There is a legend on how the Doktor vineyard got its name. It goes back to the fourteenth century, when Archbishop Boemund II was Elector of Trier. While staying in Bernkastel, where he had large vineyard holdings, the prelate fell ill. The best doctors were summoned. They came, one after the other, with the best and latest medicines of the day. And after each visit, the elector felt worse than before. As he was preparing his goodbye to this world, a servant came in with a glass of wine from one of the local vineyards to sweeten his master's final moments. The cool refreshing liquid seemed to revive him a bit and he summoned the strength to call for another, then another. The archbishop was on the road to recovery. "This," he said of the wine as he sipped, "this is the best doctor."

Other Bernkasteler vineyards: Johannisbrünnchen, Kardinalsberg, Rosenberg, Schlossberg, Stephanus-Rosengärtchen, and Weissenstein. These vineyards are in the other Grosslage (general site) for Bernkastel—Kurfürstlay.

Bianchello del Metauro, It. A fair white wine from Bianchello grapes grown in Marche, on the Adriatic coast of Italy. This wine has a slight resemblance to Verdicchio (see) but is not usually as good. Its dry, somewhat austere, flavor goes well with salt-water fish, including shellfish. It can be quite refreshing when young because of its good fruit acid. Unfortunately most Bianchello del Metauro seen here is too old.

Bianco, It. White.

Bianco Alcamo See Alcamo.

Bianco Capena See Capena.

Bianco dei Colli Maceratesi See Colli Maceratesi, Bianco dei.

Bianco di Custoza See Custoza, Bianco di.

Bianco Pitigliano See Pitigliano, Bianco.

Bianco del Rocolo See Rocolo, Bianco del.

Bianco Vergine Valdichiana See Vergine Valdichiana, Bianco.

Biancolella, It.   A grape grown in Campania in central Italy. A wine of this name, made from the Biancolella grape, is also made on the island of Ischia. This wine, which is imported into the United States, is rather heavy and coarse, and lacking in acidity.

Bienne (Biel), Sw.   White Swiss wines made predominantly from the Fendant grape, in the canton of Berne around Lake Bienne (Biel). Noted towns: Dauche, Ins, Schafis, Twann.

Bienvenue-Bâtard-Montrachet, Fr.   One of the greatest dry white wine vineyards of the world, producing golden-colored, dry, full-bodied wines from the Chardonnay grape. Its 5.7 acres yield approximately 1,500 cases of wine per year. The wines of this vineyard are practically undistinguishable from those of the Bâtard-Montrachet (see) vineyard to the south.

Bingen(er), Gm.   Bingen is one of the better and more important wine towns of the Rheinhessen (see). It now comprises not only the town of Bingen itself, but also Budesheim and Kempton. Bingener vineyards: Bubenstück, Kapellenberg, Kirchberg, Osterberg, Pfarrgarten, Rosengarten, Scharlachberg, Schelmenstück, Schlossberg-Schwätzerchen, and Schwarzenberg. Important producers: P. A. Ohler, Villa Sachsen, Staatlichen Weinbaudomänen.

Blagny, Fr.   A small hillside hamlet sitting atop the line dividing Meursault from Puligny-Montrachet. Consequently, these white Burgundies can be sold as either Meursault-Blagny or Puligny-Montrachet Hameau de Blagny.

Blanc, Fr.   White.

Blanc de Blancs   "White from whites," i.e., a white wine from white grapes. Sometimes seen on wines from the

Loire Valley. Since most white wines do come from white grapes, this phrase has little meaning (outside of Champagne) and is certainly no indication of quality.

Blanc de Cossan, It.   A highly regarded white Grenache wine from the Val d'Aosta. Although little is produced, it is worth searching for. Look for Vignoble du Prieuré de Montfleury.

Blanc de Morgex, It.   One of Italy's best white wines, from grapes grown at an altitude of about 3,000 feet in the Val d'Aosta. It is rarely seen in the United States, and unfortunately when it is, it is usually too old. This is a dry, crisp, fruity wine, light in body and with a nice touch of acid. It goes well with fresh-water fish, such as pan-fried mountain trout. Luigi Ferrando (Jacob Alessio) and Beneficio Parrocchiale (Clos du Curé) are respected producers.

Blanc de Noirs   "White from blacks," that is, a white wine from black grapes. Since most grapes give white juice, red color normally comes from the grape skins. Practically any black grape can produce a blanc de noir wine. These wines often have a tinge of pink and may be described as *oeil de perdrix* ("eye of the partridge"). Of late, California has been producing some white Pinot Noir, white Zinfandel, and even white Cabernet Sauvignon wines. The world awaits a white Alicante.

Blanc de la Salle, It.   A good, dry, crisp white wine from the Val d'Aosta. Celestino David is a good producer. This wine goes well with brook trout or other delicate fresh-water fish.

Blanc de Sauvignon   See Sauvignon Blanc.

Blanc Fumé   The local name for the Sauvignon Blanc grape around Pouilly-sur-Loire (see Pouilly-Fumé). Some California producers label their Sauvignon Blanc as Blanc Fumé to give the impression that their wine is vinified more in the style of the Loire Valley than of Graves. The Robert Mondavi Winery produces a notable Blanc Fumé.

Blanchots, Fr. One of the seven grand crus of Chablis (see).

Blanco, Sp. White.

Blanquette, Vin de, Fr. A still white wine produced from Clairette Blanche and Mauzac grapes in and around Limoux (see) in southern France, an area better known for its sparkling wine, Blanquette de Limoux.

Blayais See Blaye.

Blaye, Fr. One of the districts of Bordeaux, producing chiefly common whites ranging from dry to semi-sweet. The better ones are labeled Côtes-de-Blaye (white only), or Premières Côtes-de-Blaye (mostly red). These are pleasant quaffing wines to drink with poultry or—especially for the drier Blaye wines—with fish and shellfish.

Böckelheimer, Schloss See Schloss Böckelheimer.

Bocksbeutel, Gm. The squat, flat-sided green flagon bottle used in Franconia and parts of Baden.

Bodenheim(er), Gm. Bodenheim is one of the better wine-producing towns of the Rheinhessen mostly planted to Sylvaner grapes. Bodenheimer vineyards: Burgweg, Ebersberg, Heitersbrünnchen, Hoch, Kapelle, Kreuzberg, Leidhecke, Mönchspfad, Reichsritterstift, Silberberg, and Westrum. Important producers: Oberstleutnant Liebrecht, Staatlichen Weinbaudomänen.

Bodensee See Baden.

Bolivia No white wine of consequence is produced here.

Bolognesi dei Castelli Medioevali, Colli See Colli Bolognesi dei Castelli Medioevali.

Bolognesi di Monte San Pietro, Colli See Colli Bolognesi dei Castelli Medioevali.

Bommes, Fr. One of the five townships in the Sauternes (see) district. Vineyards: Châteaux La Tour-Blanche, Laufaurie-Peyraguey, Haut-Peyraguey, Rayne-Vigneau, Rabaud-Promis, and Sigalas-Rabaud—all first growths.

Bonnezeaux, Fr. One of the most highly regarded vineyard districts in the Coteaux du Layon (see) region of Anjou. In the best years the overripe Chenin Blanc grapes grown here are concentrated by the "noble mold" (see Botrytis cinerea). These richly sweet wines are noted for their fragrance. Best drunk either alone or with stoned fruit such as apricots, peaches, or nectarines, or with strawberries, raspberries, or blueberries. (See also Quarts de Chaume.)

Boordy Vineyard, U.S. This winery in Maryland produces an agreeable white wine from French-American hybrids simply labeled Boordy White. Other Boordy wines were made in New York State and Washington State until recently (1977). The Maryland wines always have been the most agreeable. This wine goes well with crabs and other delights from the sea, as well as with poultry and fresh-water fish.

Bordeaux, Fr. One of the world's truly great wine regions, producing a wide range of whites, from the dry Graves to the lusciously sweet Sauternes. The predominant white grape varieties are Sauvignon Blanc, Sémillon, and Muscadelle. Other white grapes grown here include Merlot Blanc, Folle Blanche, Colombard, Ugni

Blanc, and even a small amount of Riesling. The major white-wine-producing areas of Bordeaux each having its own controlled appellation of origin (AC): Barsac, Blaye or Blayais, Bordeaux Supérieur, Cadillac, Cérons, Côtes de Blaye, Côtes de Bordeaux Sainte-Macaire, Côtes de Bourg, Entre-Deux-Mers, Graves, Graves Supérieures, Graves-de-Vayres, Loupiac, Premières Côtes de Blaye, Premières Côtes de Bordeaux, Sainte-Croix-du-Mont, Sainte-Foy-Bordeaux, and Sauternes. White wine produced in a district not entitled by the wine laws to use one of these names can only be labeled Bordeaux Blanc or Bordeaux Blanc Supérieur. The designation Supérieur simply indicates a higher alcoholic content and a lower legal maximum yield per acre than those of the simple appellation. It isn't a guarantee of the wine's superior quality. These wines often are superior, however. Two major châteaux of the Haut Médoc (a great red wine region) produce white wines: Château Margaux under the name of Pavillon Blanc de Château Margaux, and Château Talbot as Caillou Blanc. Both of these wines are sold with Bordeaux Blanc AC's only since the Haut-Médoc is only officially recognized as a red wine district. Château Loudenne in the Médoc also produces a respectable white wine.

Botrytis cinerea The Latin name for the "noble rot": in German, *Edelfäule;* in French, *pourriture noble.* This is a beneficial mold which under certain conditions attacks the grapes, penetrates the skins, and causes a loss of moisture which results in high sugar levels and more concentrated juice. It also imparts a complexity of aroma and flavor. This mold is a necessary element of the great German Auslesen, Beerenauslesen, Trockenbeerenauslesen (see individual listings), the French Sauternes (see) and Barsacs (see), and the luscious Chenin Blancs from Anjou (see) and Touraine (see). Conditions encouraging the noble mold are a warm, sunny year culminating in a warm autumn with damp, foggy evenings. These conditions occur most frequently in Germany, France (Bordeaux and Loire), Hungary in the Tokaj (see) region, New York State in the Finger Lakes, and less frequently in California and other wine-producing areas. For the mold to be beneficial the grapes must be fully ripe. If they are not, even the noble mold will cause problems.

Bougros, Fr. A grand cru Chablis (see).

Bourg, Fr. A district in Bordeaux producing mediocre to ordinary white wines.

Bourgogne, Fr. Burgundy. Wines labeled Bourgogne Ordinaire, Bourgogne Grand Ordinaire, Bourgogne Hautes-Côtes de Beaune, Bourgogne Hautes-Côtes de Nuits are good, pleasant quaffing wines, best consumed when young and fresh. In poor years these wines tend to be harsh and acidic and low in fruit, but the best Vin de Bourgogne can be quite refreshing and thirst-quenching. These wines range from light to medium in body, and are low in alcohol. The grapes for these wines: Pinot Blanc, Pinot Chardonnay, Aligoté, and Melon de Bourgogne in Chablis, Côte d'Or, Chalonnais, Mâconnais, and Beaujolais (see individual listings).

Bourgogne Aligoté See Aligoté.

Bourgueil, Fr. This town in Touraine produces mostly red wines. Some whites from Chenin Blanc grapes are also made that are similar to Montlouis (see) and Chinon (see). Philippe Dauphin makes a good white Bourgueil.

Bouscaut, Château, Fr. One of the better white Graves (see).

Branco, Pr. White.

Brauneberg(er), Gm. Brauneberg is one of the better wine towns on the Mosel, producing relatively full-bodied wines with surprising power. These wines are among the richest on the Mosel, perhaps the richest of all, and in this respect comparable to those of Zeltingen (see). They are also among the longest-lived Mosels. Brauneberger vineyards: Hasenläufer, Juffer, Juffer-Sonnenuhr, Kammer, Klostergarten, and Mandelgraben. Producers of note: Ferdinand Haag, Conrad, Kirch, St. Nikolaus Hospital, Freiherr von Schorlemer, and Karp-Schreiber.

Brazil This country produces mostly undistinguished, coarse white wines that are low in acid and have spent too long in wood for the American taste.

Breganze, It. A controlled denomination of origin (DOC) producing some undistinguished little white wines in Veneto. They are generally named for the grape variety they are made from. These wines, when consumed in their youth, can be a refreshing, thirst-quenching beverage for drinking with spicy hors d'oeuvres, with fish and other fruits of the sea. They may also accompany poultry or veal dishes.

Breganze Bianco is made primarily from Tocai grapes. This wine is straw-yellow with a vinous aroma and a dry, fruity flavor. Like the other Breganze wines, it is generally low in acid, and tends to be rather soft.

Breganze Pinot Bianco, from a combination of Pinot Bianco and Pinot Grigio grapes, has a bit more character than the Breganze Bianco.

Breganze Vespaiolo is perhaps the most interesting of them all. This wine is often nicely balanced with crisp acidity. It is medium-bodied with a full, fruity flavor.

Broustet, Château, Fr. A second-growth Barsac, one of the lesser sweet wines of Barsac.

Bruce Winery, David, U.S. This California winery produces some outstanding Chardonnays.

Buçaco See Bussaco.

Bucellas, Pr. Golden, full-bodied dry wines, produced from the Arento (a Riesling-type vine) grown near Lisbon, Portugal.

Bulgaria Bulgaria does not export much white wine of consequence. The most commonly planted grape is the Dimiat (see), a variety closely related to the Chasselas. Other varieties grown in Bulgaria include Rhine Riesling, Wälschriesling, Sylvaner, Chardonnay, Furmint, Rczaziteli (a Russian variety). Hemus is a sweet Misket (Muscat) from Karlovo. Rosenthaler Riesling, from the Karlovo district, is made from a blend of the Rhine and Wälschrieslings.

Bully Hill Winery, U.S. This New York State (see) winery on Keuka Lake (see) makes a good Seyval Blanc, Aurora Blanc, Verdelet Blanc, and Bully Hill White, all from French-American hybrid grape varieties. (See also Finger Lakes.)

Burgenland See Austria.

Burger See Elbling.

Burgundy, Fr. Burgundy, in eastern France, produces the greatest dry white wines of the world, wines with few equals and no superiors. Burgundy is made up of Chablis, the Côte d'Or, the Côte Chalonnaise. Mâcon, and Beaujolais (see individual listings). The best whites are produced in Chablis and the Côte d'Or. The Côte d'Or (the "golden slope") is divided into two sections: the northern, Côte de Nuits (see), and the southern, Côte de Beaune (see). The greatest white Burgundies of the Côte d'Or come from the Côte de Beaune. The towns of Aloxe-Corton, Meursault, Puligny, and Chassagne-Montrachet produce the best wines. The white Burgundies of the Côtes Chalonnaise and Mâcon are among the best values in white wine. Beaujolais is predominantly a red-wine area, but produces some white wine as well.

The noble Chardonnay is the most important white grape variety in Burgundy. Aligoté, Melon, and Pinot Blanc are also planted. Only wines made from Chardonnay, and in some places Pinot Blanc, can be labeled with a village or a vineyard name. Burgundian wines of the lowest category are labeled Bourgogne Ordinaire or Bourgogne Grand Ordinaire, Bourgogne Aligoté, and Bourgogne. As the wines increase in quality, the geographical designation becomes more specific. Wines labeled Petit Chablis, Chablis, Bourgogne Hautes-Côtes-de-Beaune, Bourgogne Hautes-Côtes-de-Nuits, Mâcon, etc., are generally better than those from the first group. The next step is village names. French wine law recognizes premier cru and grand cru vineyards in Burgundy. A wine label with a village name followed by the words "Premier Cru" indicates that the wine came from more than one premier cru vineyard. Since most vineyards in Burgundy have multiple owners, and not all of them treat their vines or their wines equally, a producer's name is very important. Also, many owners have small holdings and sell their grapes, or in some cases their wine, to shippers who finish it, bottle it, and label it with their own (shipper's) name. So shippers are very important also. Some of the most important Burgundian shippers, quality-wise, for white wines: Louis Latour, Leroy, Louis Jadot, Joseph Drouhin, Prosper Maufoux.

White Burgundy is always dry; Chablis is the driest of all. The white Burgundies are known for their authority and strength. The better the wine, the more power it has. At the lower end of the scale, white Burgundies are dry, fresh, and fruity with a refreshing acidity and charm. They make a fine accompaniment to fish or poultry. At their best, the white Burgundies are complex wines, full-flavored and rich with a deep, fragrant perfume, a buttery texture, and a long, lingering finish.

Busa Calcara, It. A white wine produced by Lazzarini from Riesling Renano grapes in the province of Vicenza in Veneto.

Bussaco, Pr. A Portuguese wine ranging in style from dry to semi-sweet. When young it can be pleasant enough.

Cabinet See Kabinett.

Cadillac, Fr. A part of the Premières Côtes de Bordeaux (see) district producing some lightweight, sweet white wines that bear a faint resemblance to the Sauternes (see). These wines, similar to Sainte-Croix-du-Mont (see), are made primarily from Sémillon and Sauvignon Blanc grapes. Drink with fresh fruit or not-too-sweet cakes.

Caillou, Château, Fr. A second-growth Barsac (see).

Caillou Blanc, Fr. A white wine produced at the famous red wine estate of Château Talbot in the Haut-Médoc area of Bordeaux (see).

Cairanne, Fr. One of the better Côtes du Rhône villages producing some pleasant fruity whites, best consumed when young. These wines go well with veal and poultry dishes in piquant sauces.

California, U.S. The biggest state, in wine production, of the United States. From its diverse climates and soils, California produces a wide variety of wines. The California wine industry in taking advantage of the new technology—for example, cold fermentation in temperature-controlled stainless steel tanks—has been able to produce consistently good white wines. They have succeeded in making good wines from grape varieties considered rather mediocre, such as French Colombard and Chauché Gris.

Whereas each grape-growing region in France, for example, specializes in one wine or type of wine—for instance, the white Burgundies from the Chardonnay and related grape varieties—California wine regions don't make these distinctions. Different grape varieties requiring different climates and soils are planted in the same vineyard. And though certain varieties have been found to do particularly well in one subregion (microclimate) or another, the location of the vineyard is not usually specified on the label. In buying a French white Burgundy, the wine drinker knows that in general the wine from Meursault will be softer than that of Puligny-Montrachet, and both will have more depth than a Mâcon Blanc. No such distinction can be made between the Napa and Sonoma Chardonnays or those of Sonoma and Mendocino. There are regional differences in California, but thus far at least, they are less obvious than in the European wine regions. Technology and lack of tradition are factors affecting this situation.

Over all, California wines are lower in acid, and fruitier than their European counterparts. They have a softness not often found in the French or German wines.

The better wines are generally varietally labeled—named for the grape variety; the lesser wines, generically labeled—named after a famous European wine district, as if in hopes that the quality of that famed district could somehow rub off on the generally bland, mediocre little California generic. These generic wines are, by and large, soundly made, but lack character and distinction. The best feature of these Chablis, Sauternes, Rhine Wines, and Moselles is their low price. The varietal wines are a different story. Some of these wines can stand up to the best of them—California Chardonnays, Sauvignon Blancs, and Chenin Blancs. The one white grape variety that doesn't quite come up to the quality it achieves in Europe is the noble Riesling. In California, the true Riesling is labeled Johannisberg or White Riesling. The California Rieslings lack the racy elegance and remarkable fruit-to-acid balance of both the German and Alsatian Rieslings. By and large California Johannisberg or White Rieslings go well with cream dishes—chicken in cream sauce, veal in cream sauce, etc. Most of these wines range from off-dry to semi-sweet. Some of the better California Rieslings are those from Joseph Phelps Vineyard and Stag's Leap Wine Cellars. Some wineries have made lusciously sweet versions. The best have lacked the thickness and intensity of the German Trockenbeerenauslesen (see) as well as their incredible delicacy and acid balance, but they have come close in residual sugar. At their best, these wines have been quite impressive—notably those from Joseph Phelps (the 1975 and, especially, the 1976).

The name Riesling without the qualifying "White" or "Johannisberg" is almost a generic term in California. Most wines labeled Riesling are not in fact Rieslings—some are Sylvaners, and the others—who knows what. Grey Riesling is not a Riesling; it is the Chauché Gris. Monterey Riesling is the Sylvaner; Emerald Riesling is a hybrid, and so on. These wines for the most part range in style from off-dry to semi-sweet. They are a good choice to accompany fish in cream sauces, mixed seafood appetizers, cold veal, or chicken. There are many passable ones made, but none outstanding.

One white grape variety that seems to do better in California than it does in Europe is the Sauvignon Blanc, or as some wineries call it, Fumé Blanc. The better ones are quite comparable to their European counterparts. Notable Sauvignon or Fumé Blancs are produced by Spring Mountain, Sterling, Dry Creek, and Robert Mondavi. Christian Brothers Napa Fumé is quite good. Although it lacks the intensity of the others, its price makes it an outstanding value. California Sauvignon Blanc, especially in the drier style, goes well with salt-water fish and shellfish.

Chardonnay, or Pinot Chardonnay, produces the greatest dry white wines of the world, and some of them come from California. Outstanding examples are produced by Chateau Montelena, Spring Mountain, Mayacamas, David Bruce, Hanzell, and others. The better Chardonnays are a fine accompaniment to roast veal or poultry, especially turkey or game hen. The lesser Chardonnays—there are some fine values in the lower price brackets—go well with veal, pork, and saltwater fish.

The California Gewurztraminers, like the Rieslings, generally lack the acidity and spice of the Alsatian versions; they tend to be softer and rounder with higher alcohol and less distinction. Mirassou has produced some fine Gewurztraminers. In recent vintages, though, it has been leaving some residual sugar in the wine, perhaps to make a wine with more general appeal.

California Semillon isn't quite as impressive as the Sauvignon Blanc.

The Pinot Blanc is often made in a style similar to a Chardonnay, and the best can be quite impressive.

French Colombard, which is a very mediocre grape in France, produces some clean, fruity, and well-balanced wines in California. Parducci makes a good one.

Folle Blanche is bottled as a varietal by Louis Martini. Usually though, this variety is used as a blending grape.

Chenin Blanc is another very successful variety in California. Look for the dry Chappellet Chenin Blanc, which is treated almost like a Chardonnay and given wood aging. Most California Chenin Blancs have a touch of sweetness.

Green Hungarian has no true counterpart in Europe. This grape produces fruity wines with good acid balance. They are generally dry—though some off-dry versions are made—light, crisp, and pleasant. Drink with seafood or poultry in lightly seasoned sauces.

(See also individual producers and grape varieties.)

Caluso See Erbaluce di Caluso.

Canada Most of the Canadian wines are made in British Columbia and in the Niagara Peninsula, between Lake Erie, Lake Ontario, and the Niagara River. They are usually from native American grapes (Catawba, Concord, Delaware, etc.) and French-American hybrids. These wines have little to offer. Some experimental wines have been made from Chardonnay and Gewürztraminer in both areas, but little of this wine reaches the United States.

Cape Wines See South Africa.

Capena, Bianco, It. Wines produced in Lazio that are similar to those of the Castelli Romani (see).

Capri, It. More wine is sold as Capri than could possibly be made on that pretty little island in the Bay of Naples. By and large, the wine is dry, coarse, and heavy, but is suitable accompaniment to fish and shellfish in piquant sauces. A lot of the wine masquerading as Capri Bianco comes from Vesuvius and Ischia, but is no worse than the authentic stuff.

Carbonnieux, Château, Fr. One of the better white Graves (see), and reasonably priced.

Carcávelos, Pr. Fortified dessert wines from Portugal.

Cariñena, Sp. A white wine from Aragón in Spain.

Casel See Kasel.

Cassis, Fr. A dry, white, full-flavored wine produced in southern France near Marseille. It goes well with seafood dishes such as bouillabaisse.

Castel del Monte, It.   A white wine from Apulia, generally heavy, dull, and lacking charm. Drink with spicy seafood dishes.

Castelli di Jesi   See Verdicchio.

Castelli Romani, It.   These wines come from the Alban hills southeast of Rome. The best are dry, fresh, and fruity, and very light-bodied. Their biggest virtue is their freshness; they are best drunk right from cask in the local trattorias and restaurants. These wines are generally badly pasteurized when bottled, and become dull and uninteresting. They commonly finish with a trace of bitterness which becomes more evident the older the wine gets. The more highly regarded Castelli Romani wines come from the towns of Frascati, Marino, and Velletri (see).

Catawba, U.S.   A native American hybrid (a cross between Labrusca and Vinifera) producing wines low in acid, pervasively grapey, and without distinction. They are made in styles ranging from semi-sweet to sweet.

Caymus Vineyards, U.S.   A Napa Valley winery that produces a good Pinot Noir Blanc.

Cérons, Fr.   This wine produced in Bordeaux is sort of a lightweight, inexpensive Sauternes (see). It is golden in color, generally semi-sweet, relatively high in alcohol, and quite fruity.

Cerveteri, It.   This wine, produced northwest of Rome from Trebbiano, Malvasia, and other varieties, is similar to the Castelli Romani (see) wines. It is best drunk well-chilled and very young, when it is still fresh. At that time it can be pleasant and agreeable.

Chablais, Sw. One of the major wine-producing districts of the Vaud (see), upstream from where the Rhône River joins Lake Geneva. The vineyards stretch from Villeneuve at the eastern tip of the lake, southeast along the Rhône Valley. For the most part, the wines are white, dry, light to medium-bodied, simple and uncomplicated. A wine to accompany river or lake fish, or cheese fondue. Most of the Chablais wines are made from the Fendant, or Chasselas grape—here called the Dorin. The best of these wines, from the towns of Yvorne and Aigle (see), are among the best wines of Switzerland. Other good Chablais wines come from Bex and Ollon. Clos de Rennauds and Clos du Rocher are noted estates.

Chablis, Fr. One of the world's greatest white-wine-producing regions. Chablis, 100 miles north of the famous Burgundian Côte d'Or, is in fact a part of Burgundy. These hillside vineyards are planted in chalky soil. The climate is hazardous; spring frosts are a major danger, and all too often violent hailstones pelt the vines during the summer.

But when the sun smiles here, Chablis is one of the world's vinicultural treasures—bone-dry, crisp, big-bodied, and flavorful, with refreshing acidity, and distinction. This wine is perhaps the palest and driest of all the white table wines, with an austerity rarely matched. It has a kind of flintiness or mineral tang that makes it the perfect companion to oysters and other shellfish. Chablis has a refreshing quality that is perhaps unequaled, and certainly unsurpassed, in any other wine.

All Chablis is made from one grape variety: Chardonnay. French wine law recognizes four categories of Chablis, according to the part of this limited zone where the grapes were grown, their alcoholic content, and the yield per acre. The greatest vineyards—the *Chablis Grand Cru*—come from one hill (250 acres). These wines must attain 11% alcohol. The grand crus make up about 5% of all Chablis. There are seven official grand cru vineyards: Blanchots, Bourgros, Les Clos, Grenouilles, Les Preuses, Valmur, and Vaudésir, which has the highest reputation. La Moutonne is considered by authorities to be of the same stature as the seven grand crus. But this is not accepted under French wine law. Moreau is a very fine producer, and the single largest producer of grand cru Chablis, with about one-third of all the grand cru wines.

Premier Cru Chablis must achieve 10.5% alcohol and come from the 1,100-acre designated zone. There are two dozen recognized premier cru vineyards: Beugnons, Boroy (or Beaurroy), Butteaux (also known as Vaugerlans), Châpelots, Châtains, Côte de Fontenay, Côte de Léchet, Forêts, Fourchaume, Lys, Mélinots, Monts de Milieu, Montée-de-Tonnerre, Montmains, Pied d'Aloup, Roncières, Séché (also known as Epinottes), Troême, Vaillons, Vaucoupin, Vaugiraud, Vaulorent, Vaupulent, Vosgros.

The third-rank *Chablis* must achieve 10% alcohol, and along with premier cru makes up 80% of the entire production entitled to the name Chablis.

The wines in the lowest category—those labeled *Petit Chablis*—don't last long. Drink them while they are young and fresh. These wines must be at least 9.5% alcohol and can come from anywhere in the production

This, of course, all pertains to authentic Chablis, from the Chablis region of France.

Chablis Outside of Europe, in California, New York, Canada, Australia, South America, etc., Chablis is considered a generic name, and anyone who wants to label his wine "Chablis" can, no matter how absurdly unlike true Chablis it may be. The name has little or no meaning on these generic wines. A given producer's "Chablis" is likely to be drier than his "Rhine Wine," but even that isn't always the case. To further confuse the issue, while authentic Chablis is always the product of Chardonnay grapes, generic Chablis rarely contains any Chardonnay and is usually a blend of a variety of grapes, most vastly inferior to the noble Chardonnay. Also, while authentic Chablis is dry and crisp, generic Chablis is often dull and medium dry. About the only thing that can be said for certain of these generics is that they are white—that is, unless they are pink (a small amount of pink chablis is made in the United States). Maybe they would taste better if they were less pretentiously labeled.

Chalon-sur-Saône, Fr. This town gives its name to the Côte Chalonnaise (see).

Chalone Vineyards, U.S. This Monterey-based winery makes a fine Chardonnay.

Chalonnaise See Côte Chalonnaise.

Chambave, Passito di, It. See Passito di Chambave.

Chambolle-Musigny, Fr. One of the famous red wine villages of Burgundy, which does produce a small proportion of white Musigny (see).

Chappellet Vineyards, U.S. A Napa Valley winery that produces a dry Chenin Blanc with some wood aging.

Chardonnay One of the world's greatest white wine grapes.

This noble variety is also known as the Pinot Chardonnay. Chardonnay is at its finest in France and California. In France it is used to some degree in Champagne; for all authentic Chablis; for the great white Burgundies from Puligny-Montrachet, Chassagne-Montrachet, Meursault, and Aloxe-Corton on the Côte de Beaune; and for the rare Musigny Blanc and Clos Blanc de Vougeot on the Côte de Nuits. It also produces some good white Burgundies, though of lesser weight and distinction, in the Mâcon and Côte Chalonnaise areas.

In California (see) some very distinctive Chardonnays are produced, for example those of Chateau Montelena, Spring Mountain, Stony Hill, Hanzell, David Bruce, and Mayacamas.

At their best these wines go well with roast veal, roast poultry—turkey and chicken. Lesser versions go well with seafood—fish and shellfish.

Chardonnay is a low-yielding variety, which adds to the expense of these wines. Chardonnay generally ranges in color from straw-yellow with greenish reflections to pale gold in its youth, turning to a deep gold as it matures. Chardonnay has a rich bouquet variously described by experts as reminiscent of ripe fruit, peaches, figs, or green apples. A factor in the complexity of bouquet and flavor in the Chardonnay is the small oak barrels these wines are often aged in.

In New York State, Dr. Konstantin Frank (see) has produced some excellent Pinot Chardonnays from grapes grown in his Finger Lakes vineyard. Gold Seal, also of the Finger Lakes, has produced some good Chardonnays also.

Chardonnay is named for a town in the Mâcon area

of Burgundy. This town is one of the villages allowed to label their wines Mâcon Villages. This wine is similar to Pouilly-Fuissé, but is not as full or intense and has less bouquet.

Charlemagne, Fr. A grand cru of Aloxe-Corton. The Charlemagne name is rarely seen anymore as these wines are entitled to use the Corton-Charlemagne (see) name, and usually do.

Chassagne-Montrachet, Fr. One of the greatest white wine villages of the world. It shares with its neighbor to the north, Puligny-Montrachet, the highly esteemed Montrachet (see) vineyard; also Bâtard-Montrachet (see). Criots-Bâtard-Montrachet (see) to the south of Bâtard is wholly in Chassagne. In total there are about 870 acres of vines producing somewhat more red wine than white, but it is to the latter that this village owes its fame. Besides Montrachet, Chassagne has the very fine premier cru vineyards of Les Ruchottes, Morgeot, Les Cailleret, and Les Chenevottes.

Other premier cru vineyards: Abbaye de Morgeot, Boudriotte, Brussolles, Cailleret, Champs Gain, Chenevottes, Clos St.–Jean, Grands Ruchottes, Macherelles, Maltroie, Morgeot, Romanée, Vergers.

These white wines are dry yet rich in flavor, firm in texture, and have a fine bouquet and a lingering aftertaste. The village wines are perhaps more delicate than those of Puligny. These wines are a fine accompaniment to fish and poultry or, better yet, roast leg of veal.

Jean Lamy and Delegrange Bacchelet are good producers.

Chasselas A hearty, productive grape variety producing

wines that are normally low in acid and best when young. In colder climes, the grape develops sufficient acid to produce balanced wines. This variety is grown in Alsace, the Loire around Pouilly-sur-Loire (see), Germany in the Markgräflerland, in Baden (see), where it is known as Gutedel (see), and in Switzerland, where it seems to be ideally suited. Nowhere does it produce better wines than in the cantons of Valais (see) and Vaud (see) in the Rhône Valley under the name of Fendant or Dorin. This variety is used for blending in California, where it is known as the Chasselas Doré.

Château, Fr.   A French wine estate, which may or may not actually have a chateau on it. The wines are labeled "Château ..." followed by the estate name. (Wine estates labeled "Château ..." will be listed in most cases under the estate name in this book.)

Château-Chalon, Fr.   This is not an estate, but a small hilltop village in the Jura, producing a rare and unusual wine that shares a similarity with Montilla and Sherry. Like those wines, Château-Chalon develops the flor yeast, which imparts a special flavor, a kind of nuttiness, to the wine. Unlike Sherry, Château-Chalon is not fortified. This wine is made from the Savagnin grape, thought to be related to the Traminer. Château-Chalon must be kept for a minimum of six years in cask, unusual in French wine law. The casks are not kept full, and the white film of the flor develops on top of the wine. Château-Chalon is sold in a 20½-ounce stumpy bottle known as the Clavelin. This very dry, full-bodied wine is good sipped alone as an aperitif, and goes well with soups. It has an aroma reminiscent of walnuts, and is a fine after-dinner drink with walnuts, or most any kind of nuts, so invite a friend over for a glass.

Château Grillet, Fr. The smallest wine area in France to have its own controlled appellation of origin (AC). Indeed, it is the only estate to be so recognized. Château Grillet's six-acre vineyard produces a minuscule 400 to 800 cases a year. The wine, especially in fine years, can be quite outstanding. Château Grillet is pale golden in color with a distinctive fragrant perfume of flowers and spice and other things nice. It is a wine of breed and elegance. It has enormous length, finishing on a dry spicy note. Château Grillet is a fine accompaniment to simply prepared veal, pork, or poultry dishes.

Chateau Montelena, U.S. A Napa Valley winery which produces some outstanding Chardonnays.

Chateau St. Jean, U.S. A small Sonoma Valley vineyard producing a variety of premium whites, some from individual vineyards which are named on the label.

Châteauneuf-du-Pape, Fr. A wine village in the Côtes du Rhône region of France producing predominantly red wine, but some white is also made. Though often somewhat awkward, being a little low in acid and high in alcohol, at its best the white wine of Châteauneuf-du-Pape can be quite distinctive, with a spicy, fragrant bouquet and flavor. A fine choice to accompany veal or poultry in complicated or spicy sauces. White Châteauneuf-du-Pape was first made at the request of the popes at Avignon, who wanted a wine for the mass that would be less heady and strong than the red. The white today is still sometimes referred to as Vin de Messe. Some of the better white Châteauneufs: Les

Cailloux (André Brunel), Château Fortia, Domaine de Nalys (Philippe Dufays), Domaine du Christia (Etienne Grangeon), Domaine Mont Redon, Réserve du Capitole (Paul Jean), Beaurenard (Paul Coulon) and La Terre Ferme (Berard Père et Fils).

Châtillon-en-Diois, Fr.   A town near the eastern edge of the Côtes du Rhône and Die, producing a small amount of white wine that can be agreeable when young and fresh.

Chauché Gris   See Grey Riesling.

Cheilly-les-Maranges, Fr.   One of the lesser-known villages in the southern Côtes de Beaune, producing some lesser white Burgundies at fine value.

Chenin Blanc   The major white grape variety of Anjou (see) and Touraine (see) in the Loire Valley, where it is also known as Pineau de la Loire. This is also the grape variety in the wines of Vouvray, Montlouis, Saumur, Bonnezeaux, and Quarts de Chaume (see individual listings). Generally the wines made from the Chenin Blanc are soft, mellow, fruity, and off-dry to lightly sweet. Their aroma is very fruity, reminiscent of peaches. In especially fine years lusciously sweet dessert wines are produced in Anjou and Touraine from overripe Chenin Blanc grapes affected by the noble mold (see Botrytis cinerea). These wines are best sipped by themselves or with stoned fruits, especially nectarines. The off-dry Chenin Blancs go well with chicken, especially in cream sauces.

Chenin Blanc does very well in California. The best California Chenin Blancs, when young, have an engaging, uncomplicated fruitiness and charm. They are attractive and soft, ranging in style from off-dry to semi-sweet. Some good Chenin Blancs are made by Mirassou and Papagni and Parducci. Some California wineries sell their Chenin Blancs under different names, such as White Pinot, Pineau de la Loire, or Pineau followed by the producer's name. One winery, at least—Chappellet—has treated its Chenin Blanc somewhat like a Chardonnay, and given it some oak aging and vinified it dry. This wine goes well with fish.

The Steen grape variety of South Africa (see) is thought to be the Chenin Blanc.

Chenin d'Anjou   See Anjou.

Chevalier, Domaine de, Fr.   Along with Laville-Haut-Brion, this is one of the two best white wine estates of Graves (see).

Chevalier-Montrachet, Fr.   This wine is from the Chevalier-Montrachet vineyard in the upper part of the Montrachet hill—not the top, but the upper middle part (Bâtard-Montrachet comes from the lower part). While Bâtard-Montrachet is the tastier and more solid, Chevalier is the more delicate and elegant. Chevalier-Montrachet is known for its delicacy and flavor and its rich and haunting perfume. Though rich, it is dry and has incredible breed and distinction. Chevalier-Montrachet is the lightest and most delicate of all the Montrachet grand crus. This wine makes a fine companion to roast chicken or veal. Chevalier covers 12 acres, producing approximately 1,750 cases annually. Important producers: Bouchard Père et Fils, Chartron, Mme. Boillereault de Chauvigné, Georges Deleger, Jadot, Latour, and Prosper Maufoux.

Chile   Quality-wise, the best wine-producing country of South America. Though the best whites are produced from the Riesling, the Sémillon is more widely planted. Some Chardonnay is also grown, but is not often seen in the United States. Pinot Blanc, Sauvignon, and Folle Blanche are also planted. Just as in California and other parts of the New World, Chile also resorts to generic labels: Chablis, Rhine, and Sauterne. The best Chilean wines come from the central valley north and south of Santiago. Chilean whites tend to be lacking in charm, but are usually fairly priced and sometimes even outright bargains. These wines are good value to accompany steamed clams, little necks, scampi, and other fruits of the sea.

Chinon, Fr. This area of the Loire, known for its once proud medieval fortress and its red wines, also produces some good pleasant off-dry whites not unlike Montlouis (see) or Bourgeuil (see).

Christian Brothers, U.S. A California winery which produces a good Sauvignon Blanc, labeled Napa Fumé, as well as a good dessert wine, Chateau la Salle. Their Chardonnay is fair value and their Pineau de la Loire is also good.

Cinqueterre, It. This wine, so called because it comes from five villages between Genoa and La Spezia on the Ligurian coast, is rarely seen in the United States. It is made in a dry, and a semi-sweet style that is labeled Sciacchetrá. The Sciacchetrá Vino Dolce Nature is sweet.

Ciró Bianco, It. A dry, full-bodied, and somewhat awkward white wine from Calabria in the "toe" of the Italian "boot." When young, Ciró is fruity and can be agreeable. Drink well-chilled with spicy seafood or fish stews. Caruso is a respected producer.

Clairette A productive white grape variety, ranging in quality from fair to good, grown mostly in southern France. More often than not it is blended in with other varieties because of its neutral character.

Clairette de Bellegarde, Fr. A small, somewhat awkward white wine. It is best drunk in its youth in the area of production.

Clairette du Languedoc, Fr. A full-bodied, dry, flavorful wine from southern France that can be quite heady.

Clape, La, Fr. This area, east of Narbonne, produces some white wines that can be pleasant drunk with mixed seafood stews or poultry in spicy sauces.

Clessé, Fr. A village in the Mâcon producing some white wines similar to lightweight Pouilly-Fuissés.

Climens, Château, Fr. A fine, classed, first-growth Barsac (see) considered second only to Château d'Yquem (see) in quality. Climens produces a sweet, luscious, golden dessert wine known for its delicacy, extraordinary fruit, and breed.

Clos, Fr. A walled, or once walled, vineyard. This term is most commonly seen on Burgundian wines.

Clos, Les, Fr. A grand cru Chablis (see).

Clos Blanc de Vougeot, Fr. One of the small pockets of Chardonnay vines in the Côtes de Nuits. Very little of this white Burgundy is produced and it is relatively expensive.

Clos des Mouches, Fr. A premier cru vineyard in Beaune (see) which produces mostly red wines. A small amount of white, though, is also produced. Joseph Drouhin is a reliable producer.

Clos Haut-Peyraguey See Haut-Peyraguey, Clos.

Colli Albani, It. A controlled denomination of origin (DOC) which applies to the wine produced around Lake Albano south of Rome. The white wines from Malvasia and Trebbiano grapes are quite similar to the Castelli Romani (see) wines. (See Albano.)

Colli Ascolani   See Falerio di Colli Ascolani.

Colli Berici, It.   A controlled denomination of origin (DOC) for wines produced in a delimited zone of Veneto. The whites are labeled for their predominant grape variety: Garganega, Tocai, Sauvignon, Pinot Bianco. These wines are generally light to medium-bodied, dry and soft, with moderate acidity. When young and fresh, they can be quite agreeable. Drink with fresh-water fish. The Garganega is similar to Soave (see), but being less well known is a better value—not only because it is less expensive than a better Soave, but because it is also more consistent.

Colli Bolognesi dei Castelli Medioevali, It.   A controlled denomination of origin (DOC) for wines produced in the hills southwest of Bologna. The Bianco, made from Albana and Trebbiano grapes, ranges from off-dry to semi-sweet. The other whites are named for their predominant grape variety: Pinot Bianco, Riesling Italico, Sauvignon. All of these wines are medium-bodied, ranging from off-dry to semi-sweet, with moderate acidity, and are best when young, while they are still fresh and fruity. Like many Italian whites, the slightly bitter aftertaste increases with age. All go well with poultry, veal, or pasta in cream sauces.

Colli Bolognesi di Monte San Pietro   See Colli Bolognesi dei Castelli Medioevali.

Colli del Trasimeno, It.   Trebbiano, Malvasia, and other varieties grown around Lake Trasimeno in Umbria are used in this white (bianco) wine. It is medium-bodied, soft and dry, with moderate acidity. Best drunk young and fresh.

Colli Euganei, It. A DOC (controlled denomination of origin) for wines produced in the Euganean hills of Veneto. The Bianco is made from Garganega, Tocai, Sauvignon, and other varieties. It ranges from dry to semi-sweet, is light, low in acid, and rather bland. The Moscato is a sweet dessert wine often with a light sparkle.

Colli Lanuvini, It. One of the Castelli Romani (see) wines from the Alban hills southeast of Rome.

Colli Maceratesi, Bianco dei, It. White wine from Trebbiano and Malvasia grapes grown in Marche. This wine is dry, light to medium-bodied, and has moderate acidity; it ends on a bitter note. Drink when very young, while still fresh.

Colli Morenici Mantovani del Garda, It. A white (bianco) wine from Garganega, Trebbiano, and other grape varieties produced in Lombardy. It is a dry, fruity wine ranging from light to medium in body. Colli Morenici Mantovani del Garda can be pleasant drinking when young and fresh.

Colli Orientali del Friuli, It. One of the controlled denominations of origin (DOC) of Friuli-Venezia-Giulia (see). These white wines, like those from other Friulian DOC zones, are named for their predominant grape variety: Picolit, Pinot Bianco, Pinot Grigio, Ribolla, Riesling Renano, Sauvignon, Tocai, and Verduzzo (see individual listings). The most interesting white wines of Colli Orientali are Picolit, Ribolla, and Verduzzo. The best white wines here are the Pinot Grigio and

Sauvignon. All of these wines, except perhaps the Picolit and Verduzzo, should be consumed within a year of the vintage. As with most Italian whites, the younger the better. Some notable producers: Comelli, Livio Felluga, Filiputti, Conti Florio, Formentini, Gradnik, Kechler, and Russiz. Other whites produced in this zone: Malvasia and Traminer; neither recognized by DOC.

Colli Tortonesi, It. A DOC applying to wines produced in the Tortona hills of the Piedmont east of Alessandria. The Cortese (named for the grape) is light straw in color, light in body, dry, fruity, and has a slightly bitter aftertaste. Best when young with trout, pike, or other fresh-water fish.

Collio See Collio Goriziano.

Collio Goriziano, It. The white wines from this delimited zone west of Gorizia are similar to those of the other DOC zones of Friuli-Venezia-Giulia (see). White wines labeled Collio or Collio Goriziano without specifying a grape name are made from Ribolla Gialla, Malvasia, and Tocai grapes. The other white wines here are named for the variety they are made from: Malvasia, Pinot Bianco, Pinot Grigio, Tocai, Riesling Italico, Sauvignon, and Traminer. Non-DOC whites include a Müller-Thurgau and a Ribolla Gialla. Mario Schiopetto is a good producer of the former wine; Gradmir Gradnik makes a good Ribolla Gialla. Other good producers of Collio white: Conti Attems, Livio Felluga, Marco Felluga, Conti Formentini, and Villa Russiz. The Pinot Grigio and Sauvignon are the most distinctive Collio Goriziano wines; Pinot Bianco the least distinctive.

Colombard   See French Colombard.

Colombia   Very little white wine is produced in this South American country, and even less is imported into the United States.

Colonna   See Montecompatri-Colonna.

Concannon Vineyard, U.S.   A California winery in the Livermore Valley that produces a good Muscat di Frontignan.

Concord   The most widely planted grape variety in New York State. There are also plantings of Concord in Canada, Washington State, and other places. This vine is of the native American species *Vitis labrusca*. No other variety seems to typify so well the native species' pervasively grapey (foxy) character. These grapes are low in sugar and high in acid, requiring the addition of both sugar and water to produce a palatable wine. Concord is put to better use in making grape juice or jelly than wine, but there are those who like it. Concord is often used to produce Kosher wines. Manischewitz White Cream Concord is a popular white Concord wine.

Condrieu, Fr.   A rare white wine from the northern Côtes du Rhône. This lightly golden, medium-bodied wine ranges from medium dry to off-sweet. Its perfume has floral, fruity overtones and it ends on a long spicy note. This is one of the few white wines that should be served just lightly chilled as the cold can mute its fragrant perfume. Drink with trout, perch, or other fresh-water fish. Georges Vernay is a very fine producer. Château du Rozay is a fine estate. Guigal also makes some good Condrieu.

Conegliano   See Prosecco di Conegliano-Valdobbiadene.

Conseil Petite Arvine, Le Vin du, It.   One of the best white wines of Italy, produced in the Val d'Aosta. It is light, dry, fruity and well-balanced with refreshing acidity.

Constantia, S.A.   A South African wine which was famous during the nineteenth century. It is produced near Cape Town.

Corbières, Fr.   Rather an ordinary white wine produced southeast of the ancient walled town of Carcassonne in the Midi. Those labeled Corbières Supérieur or Corbières du Roussillon are better than the ones labeled simply Corbières. The Roussillon wines can be refreshing, thirst-quenching, and agreeable when drunk while still young. They go well with various seafood dishes.

Cori Bianco, It.   A white wine from Lazio in central Italy. It is a medium-bodied, off-dry to semi-sweet wine that is soft and low in acid.

Corsica, Fr.   This Mediterranean island produces mostly ordinary whites that are coarse and dull.

Cortese   A white Italian grape variety planted mostly in the northwestern regions of Lombardy and Piedmont (see Oltrepò Pavese, Gavi, and Colli Tortonesi). Generally the wines are pale, light, and fruity, and are best within a year of the vintage, while they are still fresh.

Corton, Fr.   A grand cru vineyard in Aloxe-Corton producing very little white wine.

Corton-Charlemagne, Fr.   A grand cru vineyard in Aloxe-Corton in the northern part of the Côte de Beaune. This vineyard covers 61.5 acres on the upper section of the Corton hillside. The vineyard is made up of three portions, the best in the center. Louis Latour owns half of that section and his Corton-Charlemagne can and does rival Montrachet. Louis Jadot is another fine producer, as is Prosper Maufoux. These wines are golden in color, high in alcohol, rich in flavor and extract, and have an aroma which some find suggestive of cinnamon, others of gunflint. At its best, Corton-Charlemagne has great power and authority. A fine wine to accompany roast veal or turkey.

Corvo, It. Reputedly the best white wine of Sicily. This full-flavored dry wine, produced by Duca di Salaparuta, goes well with fish in spicy or piquant sauces. Unfortunately it is overpriced.

Costières-du-Gard, Fr. Rather ordinary white wines produced in southern France.

Costozza Riesling, It. One of the most interesting white wines of Veneto in northeastern Italy, produced by G. da Schio.

Côte, La, Sw. The vineyards of La Côte are planted on steep hillsides on the northern shore of Lake Geneva between Geneva and Lausanne in Vaud (see). The La Côte wines, from the Fendant (see Chasselas) grape, are light, dry, and quite agreeable when young. A good wine to accompany fresh-water fish. Bougy, Féchy, Mont-sur-Rolle, and Vinzel are among the better towns.

Côte Chalonnaise, Fr. This area south of the Côte de Beaune in Burgundy produces mostly red wines. Predominantly Chardonnay grapes are used for the whites of Montagny and Rully and the small amount of Mercurey. Some Pinot Blanc is also planted. These wines, though often excellent value, lack the authority and breed of the white Burgundies from the Côte de Beaune. They have less of a bouquet and their finish doesn't linger as long. The wines of the Côte Chalonnaise are generally light to medium in body, fruity, and dry. They are best from about the second or third year after the vintage.

Côte de Beaune, Fr. Burgundy's "golden slope," the Côte d'Or, is divided into two sections—the Côte de Nuits to the north and the Côte de Beaune to the south. The acreage of the Côte de Beaune is nearly double that of the Côte de Nuits. The Côte de Beaune produces excellent white Burgundies, mostly from Chardonnay grapes. Some Pinot Blanc is also grown. The Côte de Beaune begins at Ladoix-Serrigny and continues south through Aloxe-Corton, Pernand-Vergelesses, Savigny-les-Beaune, Chorey-les-Beaune, Beaune, Pommard, Volnay, Monthélie, Auxey-Duresses, Saint-Romain, Meursault, Puligny-Montrachet, Chassagne-Montra-chet, Saint-Aubin, Santenay, Cheilly-les-Maranges, De-zize-les-Maranges, and Sampigny-les-Maranges.

The most important white wine villages are Aloxe-Corton, Meursault, Chassagne, and Puligny-Montrachet. At least one-third of the production in Auxey-Duresses, Saint-Romain, and Saint-Aubin is also white wine.

The other villages produce all or nearly all red wine and very little white. Wines sold as Côte de Beaune Village can only be red.

Fine shippers of white Burgundy include: Bouchard Père et Fils, Joseph Drouhin, Louis Jadot, Louis Latour, Leroy, and Prosper Maufoux. Others are listed under the individual towns. (See Burgundy, and individual town listings.)

Côte de Nuits, Fr. The northern part of the "golden slope" (Côte d'Or) of Burgundy, producing mainly red wines.

A small amount of white wine is also produced in Fixin, Morey-St.-Denis, Vougeot, Chambolle-Musigny, and Nuits-St.-Georges. All are rare and relatively expensive. (See Musigny, Clos Blanc de Vougeot, Nuits-St.-Georges, Fixin, Morey-St.-Denis, and Burgundy.)

Coteaux Champenois, Fr. The still white wine of the Champagne district. These wines are very dry and austere with refreshing acidity. Those labeled Blanc de Blancs are lighter in body. Drink with salt-water fish and shellfish.

Coteaux d'Aix, Fr. This area, near Aix-en-Provence, produces some pleasant white wines, best when young, while still fresh.

Coteaux d'Aix, Coteaux des Baux, Fr. Wines labeled thus are from a more limited area than those labeled simply Coteaux d'Aix (see).

Coteaux de l'Aubance, Fr. One of the areas of Anjou (see) producing off-dry to semi-sweet wines from the Chenin Blanc grape. In the very best years, *Botrytis cinerea* (see) will shrivel up and concentrate the grapes, and a lusciously rich dessert wine will be produced.

Coteaux de la Loire, Fr. This wine-producing region runs through Anjou and into the Muscadet (see) area. The best wines in the Anjou portion come from Savennières (see). The wines of the Coteaux de la Loire are usually less sweet than those of the Coteaux du Layon. As in the other parts of Anjou, Chenin Blanc is the grape variety used in the whites.

Coteaux de Saumur See Saumur.

Coteaux de Touraine See Touraine.

Coteaux du Layon, Fr. The most important wine-producing

area of Anjou (see) in terms of quality as well as quantity. The best wines of this region are from Bonnezeaux, Quarts de Chaume, Rochefort-sur-Layon (see individual listings), and Beaulieu-sur-Layon. The best wines, from Botrytised grapes (see Botrytis cinerea), are sweet and luscious, and high in alcohol. They are slow to mature and long-lived. The best come from dry, warm years with plenty of sunshine and cool nights, and warm days in the autumn before the harvest—conditions that encourage the formation of *Botrytis,* the "noble mold." These are the finest wines of Anjou, and the best of these are bottled under the following labels: Bonnezeaux (see), Quarts de Chaume (see). The lesser wines from this area are sold as Chenin d'Anjou or simply Anjou (see). They range from off-dry to semi-sweet. Gonnet et Ravion is a good producer.

Coteaux du Loir, Fr. One of the areas of Anjou (see) producing pleasant white wines from Chenin Blanc grapes. These wines are generally drier than those from other parts of Anjou.

Coteaux du Tricastin, Fr. This area produces some agreeable little white wines that can be pleasant accompaniment to fish or poultry in piquant sauces.

Côtes d'Agly, Fr. Sweet, fortified wines from Roussillon (see) in southern France.

Côtes de Bergerac See Bergerac.

Côtes-de-Blaye See Blaye.

Côtes-de-Bordeaux, Fr. This area, southeast of Bordeaux, is on the right bank of the Garonne River. The northern part, known as the Premières Côtes de Bordeaux (see), is quality-wise the most important area. The Côtes-de-

Bordeaux wines range from lightly sweet to sweet. Cadillac (see) is a well-known village. Côtes-de-Bordeaux-Saint-Macaire is the southern area of this zone. These wines tend to be sweeter.

Côtes-de-Bordeaux-Saint-Macaire   See Côtes-de-Bordeaux.

Côtes de Bourg   See Bourg.

Côtes de Buzet, Fr.   An area, southeast of Bordeaux, producing some common white wines.

Côtes de Duras, Fr.   Semi-sweet wines produced southeast of Bordeaux from Sémillon and Sauvignon Blanc grapes.

Côtes de Montravel   See Montravel.

Côtes de Provence   See Provence.

Côtes du Jura, Fr.   The regional name for the more common wines of the Jura (see).

Côtes du Luberon, Fr.   Ordinary white wines produced east of Avignon in southern France.

Côtes du Rhône, Fr.   This area in southeastern France produces mostly red wines, but some agreeable full-bodied whites are also produced. When young and fresh, they can be quite enjoyable with poultry, veal, or fish. Their one defect is that they are sometimes deficient in acid and therefore somewhat awkward. The best come from specific areas: Château Grillet, Condrieu, St.-Joseph, St.-Péray, Hermitage, Crozes-Hermitage, Lirac, and Châteauneuf-du-Pape (see individual listings). The next step down from these are the wines labeled Côtes du Rhône Villages, with or without a village name; then those labeled simply Côtes du Rhône.

Cotnari, Rm.   A dessert wine from Rumania.

Coulée de Serrant   See Savennières.

Coutet, Château, Fr. A premier cru Barsac (see), one of the best wines of Sauternes.

Crépy, Fr. A wine from the Haute-Savoie near Geneva made from the Chasselas grape. It is light, low in alcohol, quite dry, and pleasant. It is best when young and fresh, with trout, pike, or other fresh-water fish.

Criots-Bâtard-Montrachet, Fr. This 3½-acre grand cru vineyard is in Chassagne-Montrachet. Very little wine is produced.

Cröv(er) See Kröv(er).

Crozes-Hermitage, Fr. This controlled appellation of origin (AC) produces mostly red wines, but like Hermitage (see), some white wines from Marsanne and Roussanne grapes are also produced. These whites are medium-bodied, dry, and austere. In sunny years they tend to lack acid and be off-balance. Drink within three or four years of the vintage with poultry or fish in sauces.

Custoza, Bianco di, It. A controlled denomination of origin (DOC) in Lombardy. This wine is dry or off-dry and low in acid. It is best when young and fresh, with fresh-water fish.

Cyprus Very little white wine from Cyprus is seen in this country. Commandaria, from dried grapes, is at its best thick, sweet, and rich. Muscat Alexandria, Xynisteri, Kokkineli, Agros, and Paphos are among the more popular Cypriot wines. Most Cypriot white wines are full-bodied, high in alcohol, low in acid, and off-dry—in other words, heavy, dull, and coarse.

Czechoslovakia Most of the wines of Czechoslovakia are common, ordinary, and fast-maturing white wines. Few of them are seen in the United States. Slovakia is the major wine-producing area, followed by Moravia. Some wine is produced in Bohemia as well. Furmint and Veltliner are the more important grape varieties. Other white wine varieties: Wälschriesling, Neuburger, Sylvaner, Muscatel, Traminer, Weissburgunder, Rhine Riesling, and Rulany (thought to be the Ruländer).

Dame-Blanche, Château la, Fr. A chateau in the south-ernmost part of the Haut-Médoc, just north of Graves, producing white wine from Sémillon and Sauvignon Blanc grapes—quite unusual as the Haut-Médoc is a red wine district. Château la Dame-Blanche, therefore, is allowed only the Bordeaux Supérieur appellation of origin (AC) on its label. This wine is similar to a white Graves (see), dry, medium-bodied, and fruity. Drink wish fish, especially from saltwater, or shellfish.

Dão, Pr. This region in central Portugal produces some good-quality white wines, golden in color, full-bodied, dry yet soft, and with high alcohol. They would go well with mixed seafood stews or fish baked in a sauce.

Debröi Hárslevelü, Hn. This fairly full-bodied off-dry white wine from the Hárslevelü grape might just be Hungary's best white wine. Drink with mixed seafood dishes or with poultry in a sauce.

Deidesheim(er), Gm. Deidesheim is one of the most noted wine towns of the Palatinate (see), producing relatively full-bodied wines (for Germany) with considerable bouquet and distinction. Over half of the nearly 1,000 acres of vineyards are planted to Riesling. Noted Deidesheimer vineyards include Grainhübel, Herrgott-sacker, and Leinhöhle. Other vineyards: Hohenmorgen,

Kalkofen, Kieselberg, Langenmorgen, Letten, Mäus-
höhle, Nonnenstück, and Paradiesgarten. Noted pro-
ducers: Bassermann-Jordan, V. Buhl, Bürklin-Wolf,
Deinhard, Giessen Erben, Carl Josef Hoch, Koch-
Herzog Erben, Jos. Reinhardt, Pfarrweingut, and
Weingut Hahnhof.

Dekeleia, Gc. These are rather ordinary little wines from
Greece.

Delaware, U.S. One of the better native American white
wine grapes, having less of the pervasive grapey
quality so common in wines from the native varieties.

Demestica, Gc. Perhaps a cut above the average white wine
from the Peloponnesian peninsula of Greece. The wine
is low in acid and somewhat coarse, but is fine for
accompanying spicy dishes of poultry or seafood.

Demi-Sec, Fr. Literally, semi-dry, but it really means off-
dry.

Devite, It. One of Italy's better whites, produced by Joseph
Hofstätter in the Alto Adige from Rhein Riesling and
Trollinger grapes. This wine is delicate, dry, and fruity.
Good with brook trout or other delicately flavored fish.

Dézaley, Sw. One of the best wines of Switzerland. Dézaley
is produced in the Lavaux area of the Vaud (see).

Dhron(er), Gm. Wines from this Middle (Mittel) Mosel
village don't normally achieve the heights of those
from Wehlen or Bernkastel, but can still be quite good.
The vineyards: Engelgrube, Goldtröpfchen, Grafenberg, Grosser Hengelberg, Häschen, Hofberger,
Laudamusberg, Nusswingert, Rosengärtchen, Roterd,
and Sonnenuhr. Dhroner wines are sold under the
designation Neumagen-Dhron. Dhron is in the Grosslage (general site) Michelsberg.

Diamond or **Moore's Diamond,** U.S.   This American variety produces, even for native American grapes, rather inferior wines.

Diana, U.S.   A native American variety that tends to produce wines of inconsistent quality.

Dienheim(er), Gm.   Dienheim, in the Rheinhessen, produces soft, pleasant wines with a taste of the soil. Dienheimer vineyards: Falkenberg, Herrenberg, Herrengarten, Höhlchen, Kreuz, Paterhof, Schloss, Siliusbrunnen, and Tafelstein.

Dimiat or **Dimyat,** Bl.   A rather undistinguished Bulgarian wine, named for the grape from which it is produced.

DOC   See Italy.

Doisy-Daëne, Château, Fr.   A second-growth Barsac (see). One of the least sweet—perhaps, along with Château Filhot, *the* least sweet—of all the Sauternes.

Doisy-Dubroca, Château, Fr.   A second-growth Barsac (see).

Doisy-Védrines, Château, Fr.   A second-growth Barsac (see).

Dolce, It.   Sweet.

Dom Scharzhofberger   See Scharzhofberger.

Dorin   Another name for the Chasselas in the Vaud (see).

Doux, Fr.   Sweet.

Dragasani, Rm.   A sweet Rumanian dessert wine made from the Muscat grape. Good with nuts or fruit.

Dry Creek Vineyard, U.S.   A California vineyard that produces good Fumé Blanc and Chardonnay.

Dulce, Sp.   Sweet.

Dürkheim(er), Gm.   Bad Dürkheim is the largest wine-producing town in Germany, with approximately 2,000 acres of vineyards in the Palatinate. Good sound wines are produced here which, while not great, can be a fine value, especially when from one of the better producers: Bassermann-Jordan, Bürklin-Wolf, Karst, K. Fitz-Ritter, Stumpf-Fitz. Herrenmorgen, Hochbenn, Ritter-garten, Spielberg, and Steinberg are good vineyards. Other Dürkheimer vineyards: Abtsfronhof, Fronhof, Fuchsmantel, Michelsberg, and Nonnengarten.

Dürnstein(er)   See Wachau.

Dutchess, U.S.   A native American grape variety used often in New York State wines.

Edelzwicker, Fr.   Alsatian wines labeled Edelzwicker are made of a blend *(Zwicker)* of any of the varieties considered "noble" *(edel)*: Riesling, Gewürztraminer, Traminer, Pinot Gris, Pinot Blanc, Muscat d'Alsace, and Sylvaner.

Eden Valley, As.   This wine-producing area, southeast of the Barossa Valley in South Australia, is noted for its white wines.

Ehrenfelser   A new German hybrid grape variety.

Einzellage, Gm.   An individual vineyard—the smallest area recognized by the new (1971) German wine laws (and larger than most of the old vineyards)—as opposed to an amalgamation of vineyards: Grosslage (see). Einzellage wines must be at least 75% from the vineyard named on the label. There are some 3,000 allowable vineyard names in Germany. Prior to the new German wine laws there were nearly ten times that number. The other vineyards didn't disappear, only their names did. They have now been assigned the names of the extended vineyards in the official registry book. There is no indication on the label whether the wine is from an Einzellage or a Grosslage.

Eisacktaler See Valle Isarco.

Eiswein, Gm. "Ice wine," made from late-picked, partially frozen grapes that are pressed before they can thaw. More often than not, an Eiswein is also an Auslese (see); occasionally, a Beerenauslese (see). Eiswein, though, is more delicate and less sweet than the regular versions. Its rarity makes it more expensive, however. Eiswein is one of the predicates allowed on a Qualitätswein mit Prädikat (see).

Eitelsbach(er), Gm. Eitelsbach is one of the most celebrated wine towns on the Ruwer (see), producing light-bodied, austere Rieslings noted for their flowery bouquet and great distinction. Karthäuserhofberg is by far the most famous estate, owned by Werner Tyrell (formerly by H. W. Rautenstrauch). This 45-acre property is divided into five vineyards: Burgberg, Kronenberg, Orthsberg, Sang, and Stirn. Today because of the new (1971) German wine laws, these wines must be sold as Trierer Karthäuserhofberg instead of Eitelsbacher Karthäuserhofberg. It's almost as if by decree the town of Eitelsbach no longer exists, but has been gobbled up by Trier, perhaps in the hope that some of Eitelsbach's illustrious reputation could improve the wines from Trier (see). Another noted producer: the Bischöfliches Konvikt. Marienholz is another good vineyard.

Elbling This grape variety is planted in Alsace and Lorraine in France, in Luxembourg, Switzerland, Germany, and California in the United States. It is also known as Burger and Kleinberger. This variety produces dull, ordinary wines, neutral in taste and aroma, that are low in acid and alcohol. There are about 3,000 acres still planted in Germany, nearly all on the Mosel, but not the Middle Mosel.

Eltville(r), Gm. Eltville, in the Rheingau, produces wines that are consistently good if rarely great. In the lower to middle price range, they represent good value. The demand for them generated by this good value, though, has caused their price to rise, often into the higher price brackets. Langenstück, Sandgrub, Sonnenberg, and Taubenberg are good vineyards. Schloss Eltz, Staatsweingüter, and Freiherr Langwerth von Simmern are respected producers. Other noted producers: Jakob Fischer Erben and Dr. R. Weil. Other Eltviller vineyards: Rheinberg. Eltville is in the general site (Grosslage) Heiligenstock.

Elvira A native American grape variety.

Emerald Riesling This productive grape variety is a cross between the Muscadelle and White Riesling varieties. It does well in the warmer districts of California, producing wines that are, at their best, clean, fresh, and fruity, with a nice acid level to balance. The aroma has a slight hint of Muscat. A good wine with veal or chicken dishes. Paul Masson makes a respectable Emerald Riesling, as does Angelo Papagni.

England Some two dozen wineries in England, mostly in the southern part of the country, produce some respectable white wines. Müller-Thurgau, often labeled Riesling X Sylvaner, is the most popular grape variety. This wine is light-bodied and has a refreshing touch of acidity. Merrydown is one of the producers whose wines are seen in the United States.

Enkirch(er), Gm. The northernmost wine town of consequence on the Middle (Mittel) Mosel. Enkircher wines
tend to be rather delicate with a flowery aroma.
Vineyards: Batterieberg, Edelberg, Ellergrub, Herrenberg, Monteneubel, Steffensberg, Weinkammer, and
Zeppwingert. These wines are in the Grosslage (general site) Schwarzlay.

Entre-Deux-Mers, Fr. One of the major vineyard districts of
Bordeaux, lying between the Garonne and Dordogne
rivers. The name is a slight exaggeration—literally,
"between two seas." This district produces dry, fruity,
medium-bodied wines that are clean and pleasant.
Generally what they lack in distinction they make up
in value. Advances in technology, such as cold fermentation, are improving the quality of these wines.
Sauvignon Blanc and Sémillon are the grape varieties
used. The better subdistricts within Entre-Deux-Mers
have their own controlled appellations of origin: Côtes
de Bordeaux, Graves de Vayres, Loupiac, Ste.-Croix-
du-Mont, and Ste.-Foy-Bordeaux (see these subdistricts
in the general listing). Château de Costis and Château
Toutigeac are two good estates. These wines go
especially well with fish, salt-water fish and shellfish.
They also make a fitting accompaniment to simple veal
or chicken dishes.

Epesses, Sw. A wine-producing town in the Vaud (see).

Erbach(er), Gm. Erbach is one of the most famous wine-
producing towns in the Rheingau, partly because of the
Marcobrunn vineyard. This vineyard, part of which is
in Hattenheim, produces some of the Rheingau's most
distinguished wines. These wines have great class,
balance, fruit, and in dry years, an outstanding bou-

quet. Schloss Reinhartshausen, Staatsweingüter, Schloss Eltz, Freiherrlich Langwerth von Simmern, and Schloss Schönborn are all fine producers who own a piece of the Marcobrunn vineyard. Other Erbacher wines, while lacking the breed of Marcobrunn, can still be very fine indeed: firm, full-bodied, and well-balanced. Other vineyards: Hohenrain, Honigberg, Michelmark, Rheinhell, Schlossberg, Siegelsberg, and Steinmorgen. Grosslage (general site): Mehrhölzchen.

Erbaluce di Caluso, It. A Piedmontese wine made from the Erbaluce grape. It is a dry wine, light to medium-bodied, and with a vinous aroma. It also has good acidity, uncommon in most Italian whites. Renato Bianco and Corrado Gnavi (Caluso Facino) are respected producers. A Passito (see) version, from over-ripe grapes, is also made but its scarcity makes it rarely seen in the United States. This is a dessert wine, high in alcohol and sugar. The vintage date on the Passito is only an indication of the youngest wine in the bottle, since the wine in barrel is topped up with younger vintages. Renato Bianco and Orsolani are noted for Caluso Passito wines.

Erden(er), Gm. Erden, on the Middle Mosel (see Mosel-Saar-Ruwer), produces some delicate Rieslings with a touch of spice in the aroma and flavor, similar to the wines of Urzig (see), its southern neighbor. Erdener vineyards: Busslay, Herrenberg, Prälat, and Treppchen. Erdener wines, being not well known, generally offer fine value. Grosslage (general site): Schwarzlay.

Ermitage, Sw. A dry, medium-bodied, fruity wine from the Valais (see). It is made from the Marsanne grape used in the Côtes du Rhône region of France, but in style is more like other Swiss wines.

Erzeuger-Abfüllung, Gm.   Estate-bottled.

Escherndorf(er), Gm.   Escherndorf is one of the better wine towns in Franconia (see). Escherndorfer Lump is one of the better Franconian vineyards. Other vineyards: Berg, Fürstenberg.

Est! Est!! Est!!! di Montefiascone, It.   A rather ordinary wine which acquired its name in a rather extraordinary way. According to the story it all began in Germany, with Bishop Johann Fugger of Augsburg. In 1110, he set off on a journey to Rome for the coronation of Henry V, a long and arduous trip in those days. Bishop Fugger was of the opinion that there's nothing better for the road dust that dries out the throat than a good bottle of wine. So he sent his man Martin on ahead, to check out the inns along the way, with the instructions to mark "Est" (It is), short for "Vinum bonum est," on the outside of any inn where the wine was good. We don't know how many wines worth an "Est" poor Martin found before he arrived at Montefiascone, 50 miles north of Rome, but we know that when he arrived in that village he was so enthusiastic over the wine he found there, that he scribbled "Est! Est!! Est!!!" on the outside of the inn. Spotting this, the thirsty bishop went in to taste, taste, taste. We don't know if he ever got to Rome, but we are told that he took up residence in Montefiascone, where he lived out the rest of his years. He died there—according to the inscription on his tombstone—from drinking too much Est! Est!! Est!!! The wine has changed since those days; it used to be a

Moscatello wine, but now is made from Trebbiano, Rossetto, and Malvasia Toscana grapes. The present-day Est! Est!! Est!!! is a rather dull and uninteresting wine, ranging from dry to semi-sweet. Drink with seafood, in stews, or piquant sauces.

Eszencia See Tokaji.

Etna Bianco, It. A Sicilian wine produced in the area around Mount Etna, including the lower slopes. It can at times be rather awkward and ponderous; at its best, however, it is among the best whites of Sicily. Drink well-chilled with seafood in spicy sauces, or fish stews.

Etoile, L', Fr. A village in the Jura (see) producing some respectable white wines.

Etschtaler See Valdadige Bianco.

Ezerjó See Mor.

Faber Wines from this new German grape variety are fresh and fruity with a Muscat aroma.

Falerio dei Colli Ascolani, It. A DOC (Denominazione di Origine Controllata) wine from Marche. It is made from Trebbiano grapes with other varieties. These are low-acid wines that can be fresh and pleasant when young, especially when served well-chilled, with assorted seafood.

Fargues, Fr. One of the five villages allowed to use the Sauternes (see) Appellation d'Origine Contrôlée (see France). Major estates: Châteaux de Fargues, Rieussec, and Romer.

Faverges, Sw. A noted vineyard in the Lavaux area of the Vaud (see) producing pleasant, light-bodied, agreeable wines from the Chasselas grape.

Fehérburgundi The Hungarian name for the Pinot Blanc (see).

Fendant, Sw. The name by which the Chasselas (see) grape is known in the Vaud, Valais, and Neuchâtel regions of Switzerland.

Fieuzal, Château, Fr. A classified estate in Graves (see) producing a small amount of good white wine.

Filhot, Château, Fr. This second-growth Sauternes (see) is the least sweet of those wines.

Finger Lakes, U.S. The major wine-producing area of New York State. In terms of quality, the wines of Dr. Konstantin Frank (see) at Vinifera Wine Cellars stand out. Also notable are the Chardonnays and Rieslings of Gold Seal (see). Bully Hill (see) and Boordy (see) produce wines from French-American hybrid grapes. Taylor, Great Western, Widmer, and others produce wine from the native American varieties. In terms of variety, this area is perhaps the most diversified in the world of wines. In terms of quality, however, little of note is produced. Only Dr. Frank produces outstanding wines. There are some good wines produced at Gold Seal. Bully Hill offers some pleasant wines.

Fixin, Fr. The northernmost wine village in the Côte d'Or. White varieties are allowed, but very little white wine is produced.

Flora A cross between Sémillon and Traminer, producing some pleasant, fruity wines in California.

Folle Blanche This grape is also known as Picpoul and Gros Plant (see). Folle Blanche produces pale-colored, light-bodied, common little wines somewhat deficient in fruit and very high in acid. There are some plantings in

California, where it is used mostly for blending, though Louis Martini makes a varietal Folle Blanche.

Forst(er), Gm. Forst is perhaps the best town in the Palatinate for quality wines. These are full-bodied wines with fine bouquet and exceptional elegance, particularly those from the Riesling grape. Riesling is planted on almost three-quarters of the 500 acres of vines here. Although Jesuitengarten is the most famous Forster estate, it is not quite so fine as Kirchenstück. Other vineyards: Elster, Freundstück, Musenhang, Pechstein, and Ungeheuer. Notable producers: Bassermann-Jordan, v. Buhl, Bürklin-Wolf, Hahnhof, Carl Joseph Hoch, Eugen Spindler, Wilhelm Spindler, and Werle Erben.

France In terms of quantity as well as quality, France is one of the major wine-producing countries of the world. Burgundy, Alsace, Bordeaux, and the Loire are France's major white wine districts. White wine is also produced in some of the other regions—the Côtes du Rhône, Jura, Provence, etc. Each area of France has its few important grape varieties: Sauvignon Blanc and Sémillon in Bordeaux, Chardonnay in Burgundy, Chenin Blanc in Anjou and Touraine, and Sauvignon in Sancerre and Pouilly-Fumé. France has a long history of winemaking, and has found which grape varieties do best in which areas. This is why in those countries that don't prohibit the use of regional names from other countries—the so-called generic names—most of the "borrowed" names are French: Burgundy, Sauternes, Chablis, Claret, and Champagne. No other country has quite so many names claimed to be "types" of wine.

French wine law, Appellation d'Origine Contrôlée, governs the use (in France) of those names and others that are more specific. By and large, French wine law is the most reasonable, allowing the producers to make decisions based on changing conditions—climatic, technological, and market conditions. With few exceptions French wine law doesn't specify what percentages of each grape must be used to make a particular wine; the exceptions are mainly in those regions where only one variety is used. Nor does the law, for the most part, specify the length of time the wine must be aged, or in what type of cooperage. These decisions are left up to those who know the wine best—the men who work with it. Generally, the more specific a French wine label, the better the wine. (This is discussed in more detail under each region.) Most French white wines are food wines. There are exceptions, notably the sweet wines of Anjou, Touraine, and Sauternes. Not only do most French white wines go with food, but they are generally better with food than alone.

Franciacorta Pinot, It.   This dry, pale-colored wine is one of Italy's best whites. Baroni Monti della Corte is a fine producer. His Franciacorta Pinot di Nigoline is medium-bodied, fruity, and well-balanced, with a buttery texture. The aroma hints of almonds. Franciacorta Pinot is made from Pinot Bianco grapes grown in

Franconia, Gm.   One of the eleven designated wine regions (Anbaugebiete) of Germany. Franconian wines are similar to those from Baden and Württemberg. They are the fullest of all German wines. They go well with food, and are in fact better with food than without.

Franken wines are dry and firm with a slight taste of the earth. They are somewhat higher in alcohol than their more delicate cousins from the Mosel and Rhine, and their bouquet and character are less distinguished. These wines come in the flagon-shaped *Bocksbeutel*. Franken wines are sometimes called Stein Wine, after Franconia's most noted vineyard, Würzburger Stein (see Würzburger). Franconia is on the Main (River) Triangle, with Gemünden, Ochsenfurt, and Schweinfurt making up the three corners. Besides Würzburg, other important towns are Escherndorf (see), Iphofen (see), and Randersacker (see). Müller-Thurgau and Sylvaner are the most important grape varieties here, comprising over 80% of the plantings. Franconia is divided into four subregions (Bereich): Mainviereck, Maindreieck, Steigerwald, and Bayerischer Bodensee. In terms of quality, Maindreieck and Steigerwald are the most important. About one half of the wine of Franconia is made by large growers' cooperatives. At one time the wines of Franconia were good value, but today they are overpriced, especially the Auslesen (see).

Frank, Dr. Konstantin, U.S. The founder and owner of Vinifera Wine Cellars and the first man to successfully grow the European *(vinifera)* varieties—Chardonnay, Riesling, Gewürztraminer, etc.—in the Finger Lakes, New York State's most important wine-producing district. Originally he planted the European varieties for Gold Seal (see), then in 1962 founded his own winery. His most successful varieties are Johannisberg Riesling, Gewürztraminer, and Pinot Chardonnay. His

Johannisberg Riesling and Gerwürztraminer at their best are without equal in the western hemisphere.

His *Johannisberg Riesling* is dry, medium-bodied, and fruity with an herby-citrusy quality on the nose. This wine has an outstanding fruit-to-acid balance. Drink with fish of all kinds, or poultry.

Frank's *Gewürztraminer* also has a fine fruit-to-acid balance. In bouquet and flavor it is rich and spicy. It is generally dry, but in some years there is some noticeable sweetness.

Frank's *Chardonnay* at its best is lighter and more elegant than the better California Chardonnays. But his wine in no respect lacks fruit; it can be quite rich and full on the palate. A good choice to accompany veal or turkey.

Other fine wines made by Dr. Frank are Pinot Gris and Sereksia. This last is a Russian variety. Both of these wines are produced in very limited supply. In fact, all of Dr. Frank's wines are produced in small amounts. But they are worth seeking out. He also makes a good Muscat Ottonel (see).

Franken Riesling   Another name for the Sylvaner grape (see).

Franken Wein   See Franconia.

Frascati, It.   One of Italy's most popular light wines. Most of it, especially that which is bottled and exported, is of disappointing quality, however. Frascati can be quite agreeable when it is young and fresh. For this reason it is best drunk right from cask, in Rome and the Castelli Romani (see) where it is made. Frascati is pasteurized when bottled, which gives it a bland, lifeless aspect. One producer, Fontana Candida, holds its Frascati in

large vats at low temperatures until it is ready to be
shipped. It is then bottled and shipped in refrigerated
compartments on board ship. This helps considerably
to preserve its freshness. Frascati is the most famous of
the Castelli Romani wines. It is made in three styles:
secco (dry), amabile (semi-sweet), and cannellino or
dolce (sweet). "Superiore" on the label indicates a
higher alcoholic content. Drink the secco with poultry
or fresh-water fish. The amabile would go well with fish
or poultry in cream sauces. Nuts or fruit may accompany the sweet Frascati.

Frecciarossa, It.   Frecciarossa (red arrow) is the brand name
of wines produced by Dr. Giorgio Odero in the Oltrepò
Pavese (see) region of Lombardy. His La Vigne
Blanche, which is relatively popular in this country,
has become overpriced. It is made from a blend of
Riesling and Pinot Nero.

Freemark Abbey, U.S.   A California winery whose Chardonnays have achieved much recognition.

French Colombard   A grape variety generally producing a
high-acid wine without much distinction. Parducci, of
California, produces a good one.

Friuli-Venezia-Giulia, It.   After the Val d'Aosta and the Alto
Adige, this region produces on average the best Italian
whites. These wines, generally a bit low in acid, are
best when they are young—very young, fruity, and
fresh. For the most part, they are too old a year after
the vintage, and rarely do they reach this country
while they are still young and fresh. Angoris is one
producer now shipping in the youngest vintage possible, notably its Pinot Grigio. Friuli, in the northeastern
part of Italy, is divided into six viticultural districts:

Aquileia, Collio Goriziano, Colli Orientali del Friuli, Grave del Friuli, Isonzo, and Latisana (see under individual listings). The Friuli wines are labeled, as a rule, with one of these district names followed by the grape name. Not all varieties are recognized by Italian wine law (DOC) for each region. The important varieties here are Malvasia, Pinot Bianco, Pinot Grigio, Ribolla, Riesling Italico, Riesling Renano (Rhein), Sauvignon, Tocai, Traminer, and Verduzzo. Picolit is also grown, in the Colli Orientali del Friuli, but is very rare. Plantings of Müller-Thurgau are also found, but they are not recognized under DOC. The best variety of Friuli is the Pinot Grigio and at their best Tocai and Traminer also do well. Sauvignon, while it can be good here, lacks varietal character. Verduzzo, in the hands of a good producer, can also be an interesting wine. The sweeter styles of this wine are better than the drier ones.

Frontignan, Fr. A fortified dessert wine made from the Muscat de Frontignan grape (see) in the Languedoc. Good with fruit or nuts.

Frühroter Veltliner See Veltliner.

Fu Jin, U.S. A pleasant, agreeable blended wine from California House Winery.

Fumé Blanc See Sauvignon Blanc.

Furmint A Hungarian grape variety also grown in Austria and the Balkan countries. It is the grape used in Hungary's most famous wine, Tokaji (see).

Gabiola Bianco, It. A white wine produced by Marzio Piccinini in the Colli Bolognesi (see) area of Emilia-Romagna. These wines have no DOC (Denominazione di Origine Controllata); Italian wine law doesn't recognize wines labeled Colli Bolognesi Gabiola Bianco. There is a Gabiola Bianco made from Bura grapes, and another from Pignulein, believed to be the Chardonnay.

Gabiola Bura   See Gabiola Bianco.

Gabiola Pignulein   See Gabiola Bianco.

Gaillac, Fr.   Pale-colored wines from southern France, generally low in acid, bland, and common. When served well-chilled, they can be a thirst-quenching beverage to drink with fried fish and seafood.

Gambellara, It.   This wine is made from the same grape varieties as Soave, and is similar in taste. It is pale in color, with a perfumed, vinous aroma, light to medium-bodied, dry, and fruity with a slight bitterness at the end. As this wine is less commercially popular than Soave (see), it is generally a better buy. A good wine for fish and shellfish. Like Soave also, a dessert version is made; it is labeled Recioto di Gambellara. Drink with fruit or nuts. There is also a sweeter version than the Recioto, Vin Santo di Gambellara, but this is rather rare.

Gavi, It.   A Piedmontese wine made from Cortese grapes grown around the town of Gavi. Best when consumed very young, while it is still fresh and fruity, this wine is light-bodied and generally a bit low in acid. Serve well-chilled with pan-fried trout, pike, or other fresh-water fish. Spinola and Soldati are respected producers.

Gavi di Gavi   See Gavi.

Geisenheim(er), Gm.   The wines of Geisenheim are among the most consistent of the Rheingaus. Even in lesser years, the wines can be quite good; in great years, outstanding. The Geisenheimer wines are among the best buys of the Rheingau, as they are not as much in demand as those from some of the more famous towns, and are consequently less expensive. Geisenheimer vineyards: Fuchsberg, Kilzberg, Klaus, Kläuserweg, Mäuerchen, Mönchspfad, Rothenberg, and Schloss- garten. Geisenheim is in the Grosslage (general site) Burgweg. Good producers include Josef Berger Erben, Hessische Forschungsanstalt, Landgräflich Hessisches Weingut, G. H. von Mumm, Schloss Schönborn, Geh. Rat Julius Wegeler Erben, Freiherr von Zwierlein Erben, and C. Schumann-Nägler.

Geneva, Sw. This Swiss wine-producing district produces some pleasant wines from the Fendant grape. While not as good as those from Valais (see) or Vaud (see), the Geneva wines can be enjoyable when drunk well- chilled with pan-fried brook trout or similar fish dishes.

Germany The northernmost important wine-producing country in the world. Grapes are planted in Germany as far north as the vine will grow. Because of the cooler climate, German wines are light-bodied and low in alcohol. The grape ripens slowly here and German wines develop an incomparable bouquet. With very few exceptions, German wines range from off-dry to lusciously sweet; and the better the wine, the sweeter it is. If one characteristic stands out in the German wines it is the extraordinary balance of sugar and fruit acid. In poor years—years with too little sun and/or too much rain—these wines are harsh, thin, and acidic, lacking charm and appeal. But when the sun shines, nowhere else in the world can produce wines of comparable delicacy and balance. Just as the French wines are food wines par excellence, German wines are sipping wines extraordinaire. The appeal is in their delicacy and subtleties; food, no matter how delicate, would only get in the way. There are some exceptions: Baden, Württemberg, and Franconia produce wines that go with food. But the best Rhein and Mosel wines are best without food, with good company to help enjoy them.

At one time the German wine labels were the most informative in the world. The claim was made that they were so clear they were confusing. So new regulations arose to simplify the confusion—by making them less clear. The best German labels tell the township and vineyard the grapes were grown in, the condition of the grapes and degree of ripeness at the time of picking, whether the wine was chaptalized, and who bottled the wine. There were over 25,000 site names. It was claimed that no one could remember all the vineyard names. (Of course nobody even tried— they just remembered the ones they felt were the best, or the best buys.) Now, nobody can remember all the 2,700 legally recognized sites remaining. The elimination of over 20,000 names hasn't clarified anything, because with the disappearance of those other site names came the creation of Grosslagen (general sites). The Grosslagen encompass multiple sites and often stretch across town boundaries. Any wine from a Grosslage can be labeled with the name of any of the towns included in that general site. For example,

Wiltingen is one of the most famous wine towns of the Saar; Konz and Pellingen, among the least well known. A wine from grapes grown in those two towns can now be labeled Wiltinger Scharzberg. Scharzberg is the Grosslage encompassing those three towns (plus others). There is no indication on the label that the wine is from a Grosslage. And if that isn't confusing enough, Scharzhofberg is one of the most illustrious vineyards of Germany, and Scharzberg and Scharzhofberg are pretty similar. You might even say, easily confused. At one time Piesporter Goldtröpfchen was one of the best vineyards of the Mosel. Today the vineyard boundaries have also been redrawn to encompass other vineyards less good. With these new Grosslagen and the redrawing of vineyard boundaries, it is best to learn about German wines anew. Forget the past reputation of Goldtröpfchen and re-evaluate all the vineyards of the Mosel to see where Goldtröpfchen fits in today. The general rule in redrawing the boundaries was that no single vineyard (Einzellage) should be less than 12 acres. There are a few exceptions, but not many. To use a vineyard name, at least 75% of the wine must come from that vineyard. There is an exception: Only 50.1% of the wine need come from the vineyard if the wine is a Trockenbeerenauslese (see). Viticulturally Germany is divided into eleven regions (Anbaugebiete). These regions are further divided into subregions (Bereich) which are broken down into general sites (Grosslagen) encompassing several individual sites (Einzellagen). A German wine label at the least will tell just the region; at best it will tell the town and vineyard. The town name will precede the vineyard name and end in "er"; for example, wines from the vineyard of Nussbrunnen in Hattenheim will be labeled Hattenheimer Nussbrunnen. The German wine regions, in order of vineyard acreage: Rheinhessen, Palatinate or Rheinpfalz, Baden, Mosel-Saar-Ruwer, Württemberg, Nahe, Franconia, Rheingau, Mittelrhein, Ahr, and Hessische Bergstrasse (see regions under individual listings).

Approximately forty grape varieties are planted, mostly white varieties (85% of German wine is white). About two-thirds are Müller-Thurgau, Riesling, and Sylvaner. Plantings of Müller-Thurgau are increasing; those of the Sylvaner are decreasing. Other important varieties: Bacchus, Weiss- burgunder, Elbling, Gewürztraminer, Gutedel, Kerner, Morio-Muskat, Ruländer, Scheurebe, and Traminer. Plantings of the new hybrids are increasing. Germany's best wines are the Rieslings. At its best, this grape produces superb wines of great breed and distinction, wines with an extraordinary bouquet and flavor, rich, yet delicate, and well-balanced; wines with subtle nuances of aroma and flavor. The best of these are from the Rheingau and Mosel-Saar-Ruwer and to a slightly lesser extent the Palatinate (Rheinpfalz), Rheinhessen, and Nahe. Over three-quarters of all German wines sold in the United States are not the great German wines but the more common ones. These wines sold under shippers' labels can be quite pleasant and agreeable. The major labels seen here: Bereich Bernkastel, Bereich Johannisberg, Bereich Nierstein, Kröver Nacktarsch, Liebfraumilch,

Moselblümchen, Oppenheimer Krötenbrunnen, Piesporter Goldtröpfchen, Piesporter Michelsberg, and Zeller Schwarze Katz.

Gewürztraminer A grape variety producing wines that are quite distinctive; in fact, Gewürztraminers are among the easiest to identify. These wines range in color from medium straw to pale golden. In both aroma and taste, the wines are spicy *(Gewürz* means spice). At their best they are medium-bodied, dry or off-dry, and well-balanced, with a lingering aftertaste of spice and fruit. A good wine for highly flavored fish or poultry dishes. The bigger versions—those from Alsace—are big enough to stand up to curries. In Alsace they recommend it with *foie gras*. The most distinctive Gewürztraminers come from Alsace (Leon Beyer is a very fine producer) and from New York State (Dr. Konstantin Frank's are scarce but worth looking for). The Gewürztraminers of Alsace and Dr. Konstantin Frank are generally dry or off-dry, medium-bodied, and distinguished with a rich, spicy aroma and flavor. In Alsace the grape does best in Bergheim, Guebwiller, and Turckheim, where the wines have a unique character, a strong spicy aroma and taste, and are relatively full-bodied and dry. German Gewürztraminers tend to be lighter and with at least a slight sweetness. California Gewürztraminers are generally off-dry to semi-sweet although some very dry versions are made. There are some good California ones made but, as with the Riesling, these wines generally lack the exquisite balance found in the Alsatian, German, and New York (Frank) versions, as the California Gewürztraminers tend to be low in acid. At least one vineyard, Hillcrest, produces an interesting Gewürztraminer in Oregon. This grape variety is also grown in Austria (good), and Italy (poor to good). Some of the better Italian Gewürztraminers (also called Traminer Aromatico) come from Bolzano. Good producers: Abbazia Novacella, Cantine Sociale di Termeno, Herrnhofer, Josef Hofstätter, Klosterkellerei M▪▪ri-Gries, Schloss Kehlburg, and Schloss Schwanburg.

Givry, Fr.   One of the better wine-producing towns in the Côte Chalonnaise (see).

Glacier Wine, Sw.   See Visperterminen.

Glen Elgin, As.   One of the better areas for table wine in New South Wales. Sémillon is the most important white wine grape.

Gold Seal, U.S.   A New York State winery producing a good, reasonably priced Chardonnay and a fair-quality Johannisberg Riesling. Besides the vinifera wines of Dr. Konstantin Frank, only Gold Seal produces the European varieties in any quantity in New York State. Charles Fournier of Gold Seal was the only man to recognize the genius of Dr. Konstantin Frank in 1953, when he hired Frank and gave him the chance to prove his contention that the European varieties could grow in New York. Fournier himself believed that these grapes could do well in New York. The New York State wine industry owes an as yet unacknowledged debt to these two men. Their efforts will have done much to improve the quality of New York State wine. (See New York and Frank, Dr. Konstantin.)

Graach(er), Gm.   The wines from the small Middle (Mittel)

Mosel village of Graach are noted for their fragrant bouquet, their balance and distinction. These wines tend to be quite light-bodied even for a Mosel wine. The best-known, though not the best, Graacher vineyard is Josephshof (see). This vineyard is so famous that it is allowed to omit the town name and simply be labeled as Josephshöfer. This 25-acre vineyard is owned in its entirety by Reichsgraf von Kesselstatt. At one time Abtsberg, Domprobst, and Himmelreich usually produced better wines than Josephshof. (Kesselstatt also owns portions of these fine vineyards.) Whether they are still better depends on what the government has done to these vineyards and boundaries. The safest thing would probably be to go by the name of one of the better producers, such as Deinhard, Friedrich Wilhelm Gymnasium, J. J. Prüm, or Dr. Thanisch. Since the vineyards of Graach have been consolidated, there are now only the four mentioned above. Other noted producers: Adams-Bergweiler, Pauly-Bergweiler, Dr. Weins Erben, Pfarrkirche St. Michael, Peter Prüm, S. A. Prüm Erben, St. Nikolaus Hospital, and von Schorlemer.

Grand Cru See Grande Réserve.

Grand Vin See Grande Réserve.

Grande Réserve, Fr. The only place in France where Grande Réserve, Grand Cru, Grand Vin, or Réserve Exceptionnel has any legal status is in Alsace (see). There it means a wine from one of the noble varieties of no less than 11% alcohol. Generally the wine is fuller in body and sweeter in taste than a regular bottling. This doesn't, however, mean that the wine is sweet. It isn't. Normally it is off-dry or at most semi-sweet. The grapes are very ripe, from a late picking.

Grave del Friuli, It. One of the major wine-producing districts of Friuli-Venezia-Giulia (see). White varieties allowed under this DOC: Tocai, Pinot Bianco, Pinot Grigio, and Verduzzo. These wines tend to be dull and ordinary, lacking in acid and charm. If young enough, though, they can be pleasant. These wines are generally overpriced.

Graves, Fr. One of the major wine-producing districts of Bordeaux famous for both its red and white wines. The predominant white grape varieties are Sauvignon Blanc and Sémillon. At one time there was more Sémillon planted; today there is more Sauvignon. Technology has done much to improve these wines. The wines tend to be lighter, better balanced, cleaner, and fresher than they once were. Another improvement—the whites now contain less sulfur dioxide. The cheaper white Graves, however, are still dull and common wines with little redeeming value. The best are among the world's greatest white wines—dry, full-flavored, and well-balanced. These wines improve in the bottle, for five, ten, or even fifteen years. Drink the younger Graves with shellfish, pan-fried or broiled fish. An older white Graves goes well with fish or poultry, especially roast chicken. Wines attaining at least 12% alcohol may carry the appellation Graves Supérieures, others may bear only the AC Graves. The best white Graves: Château Laville-Haut-Brion, Domaine de Chevalier, and Château Haut-Brion. (These last two also produce highly regarded red wines.) Other good estates for white Graves: Châteaux Baret, Bouscaut, Carbonnieux, La Tour-Martillac, Malartic-Lagravière, and Olivier.

Graves de Vayres, Fr. One of the lesser districts of Bordeaux, actually part of Entre-Deux-Mers but with its own AC. These wines are no better than a good Entre-Deux-Mers (see).

Graves Supérieures See Graves.

Great Western See Victoria.

Greco di Bianco, It. This white produced in southern Italy, in the province of Calabria, can be an interesting wine. Look for Umberto Ceratti.

Greco di Tufo, It. This wine, from the province of Campania, is made from the Greco di Tufo grape. It is generally rather dull, flat, lacking in acid, and uninteresting. It is usually overpriced.

Greece The white wines of Greece are generally common, coarse, and awkward, being high in alcohol and low in acid. The best whites come from Peloponnese and Attica. Look for Santa Helena from the former district and Hymettus from the latter. Drink these wines well-chilled with oily or spicy seafood dishes. A dry Lindos wine is produced on the island of Rhodes, and on Samos some good Muscats. The one wine that seems to typify Greece, though, is Retsina (see), a white wine (also rosé) flavored with pine resin. Definitely an acquired taste.

Green Hungarian, U.S. This California grape variety generally produces some common wines made in a light-bodied, off-dry style. The wines can be pleasant and agreeable. Drink with chicken in light sauces or fresh-water fish. It is fine for picnics and parties as it is simply a quaffing wine.

Grey Riesling, U.S. This is the name given to the Chauché Gris grape in California. It is not a Riesling. The wines produced can be enjoyable, as they are soft and fruity, although a little dull. Drink with fish and poultry dishes.

Gribianco, It. A wine from Grignolino grapes vinified in white produced by Ermenegildo Leporati.

Grillet, Château See Château Grillet.

Grinzing(er), Au. Grüner Veltliner, Riesling, and Sylvaner are the predominant grape varieties of this wine district, a suburb of Vienna. The best of the Grinzinger wine is bottled and can be quite agreeable. Generally very reasonably priced.

Grk, Yg. A dry white wine from Dalmatia in Yugoslavia (see).

Gros Plant, Fr. This grape, also known as Folle Blanche, produces high-acid wines in the region around Nantes in Brittany, from whence Muscadet (see) also comes. At one time this wine was quite inexpensive; today, at least for those bottles available in this country, it is overpriced. Drink well-chilled with fish or shellfish.

Grosslage, Gm. A general site name, usually encompassing a few individual vineyards. No indication is given on the label whether the wine comes from a Grosslage or an individual vineyard. Some Grosslagen have taken the names of what were formerly highly regarded individual vineyards. For example, Rehbach and Auflangen in Nierstein are now both Grosslagen. Today a wine labeled Niersteiner Rehbach or Niersteiner Auflangen will come from one or more sites in Nierstein that are less highly regarded than Rehbach or Auflangen were. And, only 75% of the wine must come from the named Grosslage.

Grüner Veltliner See Veltliner.

Guiraud, Château, Fr. A first-growth Sauternes (see).

Gumpoldskirchen(er), Au. The best-known wine-producing town of Austria. Generally of good value, these wines are light, fruity, and pleasant, with a refreshing acidity and a dry flavor. Gumpoldskirchener is a good wine to accompany trout, pike, perch, or other fresh-water fish; it also goes well with cold veal.

Gutedel Wines from this grape variety are light, neutral in flavor, and low in alcohol and acid. They are best drunk very young. Of the 3,000 acres planted in Germany nearly all is grown in the Markgräflerland district of Baden. Gutedel is the German name for the Chasselas or Fendant grape.

Hallgarten(er), Gm. Hallgarten is set back from the Rhine, just behind Hattenheim. Its wines are perhaps the fullest-bodied of the Rheingau wines, and among the driest. Hallgartener vineyards: Hendelberg, Jungfer, Schönhell, and Würzgarten. Hallgarten is in the Grosslage (general site) Mehrhölzchen. Important producers: Karl Franz Engelmann, Fürstlich Löwenstein, Geh. Rat Julius Wegeler Erben.

Hanzell Vineyards, U.S. Makers of a fine Chardonnay, among California's best.

Hárslevelü See Badacsony.

Hattenheim(er), Gm. The wines of Hattenheim, at their

best, have great breed and distinction tending toward delicacy rather than strength. These wines, in great years, are unsurpassed and with few equals in the Rheingau. The finest vineyard in Hattenheim, and some would say in Germany, is Steinberg (see). A piece of Marcobrunn is in Hattenheim. Other great vineyards: Nussbrunnen and Wisselbrunn. The other allowable vineyard names: Engelmannsberg, Hassel, Heiligenberg, Mannberg, Pfaffenberg, and Schützenhaus. Hattenheim is in the Grosslage (general site) Deutelsberg. Noted Hattenheimer producers: Schloss Schönborn, Schloss Reinhartshausen, Langwerth von Simmern, Staatsweingüter.

Haut Benauge, Fr. Among the more interesting white Bordeaux wines, quite similar to those of Entre-Deux-Mers (see).

Haut-Brion, Château, Fr. One of the world's most highly esteemed red wine châteaux, which also produces a small amount of white Graves. Though also highly regarded, the white is not so good as that of Château Laville-Haut-Brion (see) or Domaine de Chevalier (see), and is therefore overpriced.

Haut-Peyraguey, Clos, Fr. A first-growth Sauternes (see) from Bommes with very small production.

Haut Sauterne, U.S. This term is used as a generic name in California. It indicates simply that the wine is sweet, or at least semi-sweet, no more.

Haut-Sauternes, Fr. This term has no legal status in French wine law. It is generally used to indicate a higher quality of a particular shipper's regional Sauternes.

Heitz Cellars, U.S. The Heitz Chardonnays are among the better Chardonnays produced in California.

Hermitage, Fr. Hermitage is perhaps better known for its red wines, but some very fine white wines are also produced in this area of the Côtes du Rhône, from Marsanne and Roussanne grapes. White Hermitage is a full-bodied wine that is dry and fruity. Sometimes it lacks acid, especially in warmer years, which makes it somewhat awkward. Happily, those years are not all that common. White Hermitage is one of the longest-lived of all the dry white wines. These wines would go well with pork or turkey. The best white Hermitage is Chapoutier's Chante Alouette. Paul Jaboulet's Chevalier de Sterimberg isn't far behind. Chave also makes a good white Hermitage. Chapoutier's regular Hermitage Blanc is also good. (See also Paille, Vin de.)

Hessia See Rheinhessen.

Hessische Bergstrasse, Gm. The smallest of the eleven wine-growing regions (Anbaugebiete) of Germany, with less than 700 acres of vines. Riesling comprises over half the plantings. Müller-Thurgau and Sylvaner together make up nearly one-third. These wines are rarely seen outside of Germany.

Hochheim This name is believed to have been originally used for the wines of Hochheim (Hock, for short), supposedly a favorite of Queen Victoria, and to have been extended to encompass Rhine wines in general. Sometimes American wines are called "Hock." And this term has as much meaning as American "Rhine" wines—very little.

Hochheim(er), Gm. Although the town of Hochheim lies to the east of the Rheingau proper, it is included as part of that district. It is actually on the Main River, not the Rhine. The best wines of Hochheim are full-bodied,

well-balanced, fruity, and soft. The lesser Hochheimers
tend to be rather common, with earthy undertones on
the aroma and flavor. The most well-known vineyard in
Hochheim is Königin-Victoria-Berg, which was named
in honor of Queen Victoria, who visited the vineyard in
1850. Weingut Königin-Victoria-Berg owns the entire
15-acre vineyard. Important producers: Geh. Rat
Aschrott, Domdechant Werner'sche Weingut,
Wilhelm Fischle Erben, Schloss Schönborn, Langwerth
von Simmern, Staatsweingüter, and Weingut der Stadt
Frankfurt. Other Hochheimer vineyards: Berg, Dom-
dechaney, Herrnberg, Hofmeister, Hölle, Kirchenstück,
Reichesthal, Sommerheil, Stein, and Stielweg.
Hochheim is in the Grosslage (general site) Daubhaus.

Hungary Qualitatively, the best white wine districts of
Hungary are Tokaj-Hegyalja, Badacsony (see), Balaton-
füred-Csopak, and Somló (see). Balaton (see), Bükkalja,
Mátraalja, Mecsek, and Mór-Császár (see Mór) also
produce some good white wines. The most important
white grape varieties grown in Hungary: Furmint,
Hárslevelü, Kéknyelü, Rizling or Olaszrizling,
Veltellini (the Grüner Veltliner of Austria), Ezerjó,
Leányka, Muskotály (Muscatel), and Szürkebarát
(Pinot Gris). Also planted are Fehérburgundi (Pinot
Blanc) and Szilváni (Sylvaner). Hungary's most highly
esteemed wine is Tokaji Eszencia, followed by Tokaji
Aszu (see Tokaji). Other white wines from Hungary
available in the United States: Badacsonyi Szürkebarát
(see), Debröi Hárslevelü (see), Badacsonyi Kéknyelü
(see), Egri Leányka, Tokaji Szamorodni, Tokaji Furmint. A Hungarian wine label generally gives a district

or town name followed by a grape name. The town or district name has an "i" suffix (just as German town names have an "er" added). Unfortunately, most Hungarian whites seen here are too old. They tend to be oxidized and are rarely good. They are generally overpriced as well, making them poor value besides.

Hunter River Valley, As.   One of the better wine-producing districts of New South Wales in Australia (see). Major white varieties: Sémillon (or Hunter Valley Riesling), Blanquette, and Ugni Blanc.

Hunter Valley Riesling   Another name, in Australia, for the Sémillon.

Huxelrebe   A new German hybrid grape variety from a Weisser X Gutedel X Courtillier cross. Over 1,200 acres of Huxelrebe are planted in Germany. The wines are full and fruity with a slight hint of Muscat in the aroma.

Hybrid   This term generally refers to the French-American hybrids—grape varieties resulting from crosses between European and native American varieties. The most popular white French-American hybrid is Seyval Blanc (see). There are also hybrids (technically known as metis) from crosses between two or more European varieties, such as Emerald Riesling, Flora, Müller-Thurgau, Scheurebe, etc. (see individual listings). The intent is to produce a grape variety that will overcome the deficiencies in existing varieties. The intent in crossing the native American with European varieties, for example, was to produce plants that would be resistant to phylloxera (a root louse that was devastating the European vines) and yet not have the pervasive grapey (foxy) aroma and taste of the American grapes. The better hybrids resulting from these crossings succeed in that they don't have the foxiness, but they miss the boat as regards their resistance to phylloxera.

Hymettus, Gc. A rather indifferent, medium-bodied, dry white wine from Attica in Greece. Drink with fish or seafood in casseroles or spicy sauces.

Ihringen(er), Gm. Ihringen is one of the major wine-producing towns of the Kaiserstuhl (see Kaiserstuhl-Tuniberg) district of Baden (see). It is noted for its Ruländer wines. Ihringener vineyards: Castellberg, Doktorgarten, Fohrenberg, Kreuzhalde, Schlossberg, Steinfelsen, and Winklerberg. Grosslage (general site): Vulkanfelsen.

Iphofen(er), Gm. Iphofen is one of the better wine-producing villages of Franconia (see). Iphofener vineyards: Julius-Echter-Berg, Kalb, and Kronsberg. Juliusspital is a major producer.

Ischia, It. This medium-yellow, dry white wine, though often coarse, can be pleasant, especially when very young and fresh. Much Ischia wine is sold on its more famous sister island, Capri, as Capri wine.

Isonzo, It. One of the major wine-producing districts in Friuli-Venezia-Giulia (see) that has been granted a controlled denomination of origin (DOC). White wines covered under the DOC: Tocai, Sauvignon, Malvasia Istriana, Pinot Bianco, Pinot Grigio, Verduzzo Friulano, Riesling Renano, and Traminer Aromatico. For the most part these wines should be drunk within a year of bottling, the younger the better. Generally all varieties are a little low in acid and, though not high in alcohol, seem a bit awkward. This is not always the case, though. The best variety is Pinot Grigio. Angoris is a good name to look for. Angoris also produces a respectable Traminer. Unfortunately, the Isonzo wines are generally too old when sold in the United States, and their charm lies in their youthful fruitiness and freshness, which they quickly lose. Serving: Malvasia Istriana, as an aperitif; Pinot Bianco, with simple veal dishes; Pinot Grigio, with shellfish; Riesling Renano, fresh-water fish such as trout, bass; Sauvignon, poultry or veal dishes; Tocai, salt-water fish; Traminer, spicy fish dishes; and Verduzzo, fish or poultry.

Israel The wines of Israel are labeled (1) generically, with famous European place names, (2) with proprietary names, and (3) varietally, for the name of the predominant grape variety the wine is made from. Muscat Alexandria, Muscat de Frontignan, Clairette, Sémillon, Sauvignon Blanc, Chenin Blanc, French Colombard, and Ugni Blanc vines are planted. In general, white Israeli wines tend toward the sweeter end of the scale. And they tend, like most wines produced in hot climates, to be deficient in acid. Wines from the Carmel Wine Company cooperative are available in the United States. They produce a respectable Sémillon and Sauvignon Blanc.

Italy Italy is the largest wine producer in the world. Some outstanding red wines are produced in Italy, but very few white wines of note. Italy's whites tend to be deficient in acid, somewhat awkward, and undistinguished. Quite often they, especially the more commercial ones—such as Frascati, Orvieto, Soave, and Verdicchio—have been badly pasteurized, leaving a wine without much character that gives the impression of having been cooked. Also, most Italian whites are offered for sale in this country well past their prime. But there are exceptions, and these exceptions can be quite charming and delightful. Enough of the better ones are being offered here that they are worth looking for, including some of the more commercial ones: Frascati, Soave, and Verdicchio (see individual listings). But the better ones are in the minority. Italy is divided into twenty regions. Two regions produce the best of the Italian whites: Trentino-Alto Adige (see Alto Adige and Trentino) and the Val d'Aosta (see). Another region, Friuli-Venezia-Giulia (see), produces some respectable whites as well, particularly when they are still within a year of the vintage. All of these regions are in the mountains and foothills of the north. Some of the other regions produce some good whites also—Lombardy, for example, with Franciacorta (see)—but they are less frequent. Italian wines are usually named for their area of production—a town or district—or after the grape variety they are made from, or a combination of the two, such as Alto Adige Pinot Grigio. Occasionally they have fantasy names, such as Lachrima Christi ("tears of Christ"). Italian wine law, Denominazione di Origine Controllata (DOC), governs the production of DOC wines from the vineyard to the bottle. But the best guarantee of quality is still a reliable producer. Italian white wines are, by and large, wines for food, not sipping wines (like the German wines, for example). And, as a rule, the younger they are, the better by far.

Jasnières, Fr. A small subdistrict of Touraine (see) producing wines from the Chenin Blanc grape, generally light-bodied and medium dry.

Johannisberg, Sw. A Swiss wine made from the Sylvaner (!) grape.

Johannisberg Riesling Another name for the true Riesling (see).

Johannisberg(er), Gm. Johannisberg is perhaps the most famous wine town in the Rheingau, giving its name to the wines of the noble Riesling grape—the "Johannisberg Riesling" of the United States and other countries. Its most famous estate is Schloss Johannisberg (see). Johannisberg is the subdistrict (Bereich) name for the entire Rheingau—wines from anywhere in the Rheingau can be labeled Bereich Johannisberg. Johannisberger vineyards: Goldatzel, Hansenberg, Hölle, Klaus, Mittelhölle, Schwarzenstein, and Vogelsang. The wines from these vineyards are lesser versions of Schloss Johannisberger. They have distinction and delicacy, but not to the same extent. Some reputable producers: Geh. Rat Julius Wegeler Erben, Geromont, Jakob Hamm, Landgräflich-Hessisches, G. H. v. Mumm, and Schloss Schönborn.

Johannisberg(er), Schloss, Gm. Without question one of the most illustrious names, not only of the Rheingau, but of Germany. This 86-acre vineyard is world famous for wines of great distinction and breed. They tend to be delicate for a Rheingau, being more graceful than powerful. The entire estate is owned by the Fürst von Metternich. According to legend it was at Schloss Johannisberg that the great sweet wines from grapes affected by *Botrytis cinerea* (see) were first made. It seems that, in 1755, the messenger sent by the Bishop of Fulda, with the order to begin the harvest was captured by a band of robbers who failed to appreciate his rush. When he finally arrived the grapes were rotting on the vines, but were picked, with misgivings, and when the wine was made, it was nectar of such distinction that, weather permitting, these wines have continued to be made since despite risk and expense. (See Auslese; Beerenauslese; Trockenbeerenauslese.)

Josephshof(er), Gm. Josephshof is the most famous vineyard in Graach (see), so famous that the wines are labeled with the vineyard name only, omitting the name of the town. This 25-acre vineyard is entirely owned by Reichsgraf von Kesselstatt. Josephshöfer wine has a fine bouquet, is full-bodied, well-balanced, and is famed for its richness.

Jura, Fr. A wine-producing region in the Jura Mountains of eastern France producing a variety of wines including the unusual Vin Jaune (see) and Vin de Paille (see Paille, Vin de). Arbois (see) is one of the better villages.

Jurançon, Fr. This area in the Pyrenees is famous for its golden dessert wine. This wine has a fragrant aroma that some describe as musky, some as foxy (meaning strongly grapey, similar to the foxiness in the wines from native American grape varieties). It is a long-lived wine. In exceptional years the grapes are reputedly affected by the "noble mold" (see Botrytis cinerea). Drink with fresh fruit or nuts after dinner.

Kabinett, Gm. The lowest classification of Qualitätswein mit Prädikat (see), also the least sweet. These wines are off-dry.

Kaefferkopf, Fr. A vineyard in the Alsatian town of Ammerschwihr, famous for its Rieslings and Gewürztraminers. (See Alsace.)

Kaiserstuhl, As. The brand name of the Barossa Valley cooperative of South Australia. They produce some very good Rhine Rieslings labeled with individual vineyard names and bearing a gold label. These wines are among Australia's best whites.

Kaiserstuhl-Tuniberg, Gm. One of the major subdistricts (Bereich) of Baden (see), producing some excellent wines from the Ruländer grape (see), in fact the best Ruländers of Germany. These wines go well with delicate dishes such as fresh-water fish and roast chicken. The better wine towns include Achkarren, Bötzingen, Eichstetten, Endingen, Ihringen (see), and Jechtingen.

Kallstadt(er), Gm. Kallstadt, in the Palatinate (see), produces some good Rieslings, often at good value. Kallstadter vineyards: Annaberg, Horn, Kirchenstück, Kreidkeller, Kronenberg, Nill, and Steinacker. Stumpf-Fitze'sches Weingut Annaberg and Ruprecht are reliable producers.

Kanzem(er), Gm. Kanzem is a noted wine-producing town in the Saar (see). Kanzemer vineyards: Altenberg,

Hörecker, Schlossberg, and Sonnenberg. Bischöfliches Priesterseminar and Vereinigte Hospitien are noted producers.

Kanzler A new German hybrid, from a Müller-Thurgau X Sylvaner cross, producing aromatic wines.

Kasel(er) Gm. Kasel, on the Ruwer (see), produces Rieslings known for their bouquet and charm. Kaseler vineyards: Dominikanerberg, Herrenberg, Hitzlay, Kehrnagel, Nieschen, Paulinsberg, and Timpert. They are in the general site (Grosslage) Römerlay; the subregion (Bereich) Saar-Ruwer. Bischöfliches Priesterseminar, Bischöfliches Konvikt, and Reichsgraf von Kesselstatt are good producers. Kasel-Stadt is a different town, on the Saar, and the wines are in no way equal to those from Kasel.

Kayserberg, Fr. An Alsatian wine town producing some fine Rieslings and Gewürztraminers.

Kéknyelü, Hn. See Badacsony.

Kerner A German hybrid grape, from a Trollinger X Riesling cross, producing hearty wines with overtones of Muscat.

Keuka Lake, U.S. One of the Finger Lakes in western New York State. Dr. Konstantin Frank (see) and Gold Seal Winery (see) grow and produce some good to very fine Johannisberg Riesling, Chardonnay, Gewürztraminer, and other wines in this region. The Bully Hill Winery, in Hammondsport at the southern end of the lake, specializes in French-American hybrid varieties. Taylor and Great Western produce wines mainly from the native American varieties. At the northern end of Lake Keuka, at Penn Yan, Boordy (up until 1977) produced wines from French-American hybrids. Quality-wise, Dr. Konstantin Frank gets the nod. (See also Boordy.)

Kiedrich(er), Gm. Kiedrich, in the Rheingau, not as well known as its eastern neighbor Rauenthal or Hallgarten to the west, produces nonetheless some wines of excellent value. Noted producers: Schloss Eltz, Schloss Groensteyn, Schloss Reinhartshausen, the Staatsweingüter, and Dr. Weil. Vineyards: Gräfenberg, Klosterberg, Sandgrub, and Wasseros. Kiedricher wines are lively, fruity, and spicy.

Kleinberger See Elbling.

Klevner Another name for the Pinot Blanc (see). This grape variety is grown in Alsace, Germany, and Austria (see individual listings).

Klingelberger See Riesling; Baden.

Knipperlé A grape variety, sometimes called Räuschling, producing full-bodied wines that are rather dull and uninteresting. It is grown in Alsace, Switzerland, and Germany.

Kokineli, Gc. One of the better white Greek wines, dry and full-bodied. A good match for fish stews, mixed or spicy seafood dishes.

Königsbach(er), Gm. Königsbach is a town in the Palatinate that produces a lot of Riesling. Reichsrat von Buhl is a good producer. Vineyards: Idig, Jesuitengarten, Olberg, and Reiterpfad. Some have described the Königsbacher wines as lesser versions of those from its more illustrious neighbor, Ruppertsberg (see). That is indeed saying something. Fine value.

Krems(er), Au. One of Lower Austria's better and more noted wine-producing towns as well as a district in

Lower Austria. The major varieties: Grüner Veltliner, Rhine Riesling, Neuburger, Müller-Thurgau.

Kreuznach(er), Gm. Bad Kreuznach is the most important wine town on the Nahe (see) and one of the three best. Ten miles upstream from Bingen, it is the center of the Nahe wine trade. Bad Kreuznach is also one of the two subregions (Bereich) of the Nahe. A wine labeled Bereich Kreuznacher need not, and most likely doesn't, come from Bad Kreuznach. There are nearly forty individual vineyards, some of which are not in Bad Kreuznach but in some of the surrounding villages, that can no longer label their wines with their own village names, but must label them Kreuznacher; Winzenheim is one. Some of the better Kreuznacher vineyards: Brücken, Brückes-Treppchen, Forst, Hinkelstein, Kahlenberg, Kronenberg, Krötenpfuhl, Mollenbrunnen, Mönchberg, Mühlenberg, Narrenkappe, Osterhölle, St. Martin, and Steinweg. Noted producers: Carl Andres, August Anheuser, Paul Anheuser, Carl Finkenauer, Reichsgräflich von Plettenberg, Rudolf Anheuser, Staatsweingut Weinbaulehranstadt, Weingut Gutleuthof, and Weingut Herf und Engelsmann Erben.

Kröv(er), Gm. Kröv, producing some rather ordinary Mosel wines, is famous for its Kröver Nacktarsch ("bare bottom") wine, depicting on the label a little boy being spanked for tasting the wines in the cellar.

Labrusca, U.S. A species of North American grape varieties. This name is often used to refer collectively to all the native American varieties. Concord, which is in fact a member of the Labrusca tribe, best typifies what is meant by Labrusca. This variety, like most (if not all) American varieties, is a table grape, not really a wine grape. The wines made from these grapes have a pervasive grapey aroma and taste referred to as foxy, for being as wild as the fox, apparently because these grapes grew wild in North America. The most common native varieties used for wines: Catawba, Delaware, Diana, Dutchess, Elvira, Missouri Riesling, Niagara, Noah, Ontario, and Ripley (believe it or not).

Lachrima Christi, It. A rather coarse, full-bodied white wine from the slopes of Mount Vesuvius in the Campania region of Italy. Lachrima Christi—literally, "tears of Christ"—derives its name from a rather interesting tale. It seems that when Lucifer was thrown out of heaven, he grasped a piece of paradise which, as he fell, dropped into the Bay of Naples. One day Christ looked down at this lovely land and saw that the people were sinning. This made him sad, and he shed a tear which fell on the vineyards on the slopes of Mount Vesuvius. This touch of divine intervention improved the wines immensely, or so the story goes. Drink well-chilled with pasta in clam or mussel sauce, spicy fish and shellfish dishes.

Lacrima Christi See Lachrima Christi.

Lacryma Christi See Lachrima Christi.

Lafaurie-Peyraguey, Château, Fr. A first-growth Sauternes from the village of Bommes.

Lage, Gm. A site, or single vineyard. (See Einzellage; Grosslage.)

Lamothe, Château, Fr. A second-growth Sauternes (see).

Languedoc, Fr. This southern French region produces

mostly common white wines lacking distinction. Some good Muscats are produced at Frontignan and Lunel.

Laški Riesling The name by which the Wälschriesling is known in Yugoslavia and some of the other Balkan countries.

Latisana, It. One of the six major wine-producing zones of Friuli-Venezia-Giulia (see). The white wines under controlled denomination of origin (DOC) are Pinot Bianco, Pinot Grigio, Tocai Friulano, and Verduzzo Friulano. These wines, which tend to be awkward and low in acid, are best within a year—or, in better years, two years—of the vintage; the fresher, the better. Generally the Tocai and Pinot Bianco are undistinguished little wines, often overpriced. The Pinot Grigio and Verduzzo, when young, can be pleasant and interesting.

Lavaux See Vaud.

Laville-Haut-Brion, Château, Fr. This fine white Graves (see) is not only one of the smallest in terms of production, but one of the best in quality. It is the white wine of Château La Mission-Haut-Brion. This is a fine wine to accompany fine veal, poultry, or seafood dishes.

Layon, Coteaux du See Coteaux du Layon.

Leányka See Hungary.

Liebfrauenstift, Gm. This 26-acre vineyard in Worms (see) is believed to have given its name to the Liebfraumilch wines. The vineyard is owned by three producers—Langenbach, Heyl zu Herrnsheim, and Valckenberg, this last producer being the oldest and largest. The Liebfrauenstift wine is generally of fair quality. It is not allowed to use the Liebfraumilch name.

Liebfraumilch, Gm. This name, meaning "milk of the blessed mother," is used for blended wines, ranging in quality from poor to good. No Liebfraumilch is great, but the best can be pleasant and enjoyable. Most Liebfraumilch is mediocre at best. The only reliable guide to buying is the name of the shipper; this is a shippers' wine. The most famous is Sichel's Blue Nun. Dienhard's Hans Christof, Goldener Oktober, Hallgarten's Kellergeist and Langenbach's Crown of Crowns are other well known brands. Generally all Liebfraumilch is overpriced. Liebfraumilch can today come from any of the following districts: Rheinhessen, Rheingau, Palatinate, and Nahe. Drink with poultry, fresh-water fish (such as trout au bleu) or flounder.

Limoux, Fr. A dry white wine from the south of France. It ranges from light to medium-bodied, and while not exciting, can be pleasant. Drink young and well-chilled with fish stews (such as bouillabaisse), baked fish, or poultry in sauces

Liquoroso, It. Fortified wine, often sweet or semi-sweet. Brandy is added to stop the fermentation, thereby preserving some of the sugar. This results in a sweetish wine of 17% or more alcohol.

Lirac, Fr. A wine from the southern Côtes du Rhône. Lirac white has a vinous aroma and taste, is medium to full-bodied, and perhaps a little low in acid. When consumed young and chilled, especially with veal or poultry in piquant sauces, this wine can be quite enjoyable. Château St.-Roch produces a good white Lirac.

Ljutomer See Lutomer.

Locorotondo, It. This rather ordinary wine from southern

Italy is often shipped north for blending or to be turned into Vermouth. It is a bit surprising that such a wine should have been granted a controlled denomination of origin (DOC), especially since many of Italy's best white wines have not (see Val d'Aosta).

Loire, Fr.   One of the major white wine regions of France, named for France's longest river, flowing from the Massif Central to the Atlantic Ocean near Nantes. Along its 600-plus-mile journey the Loire waters the vines of the Lower Loire—Sancerre (see), Pouilly-Fumé cf. (see), Touraine (see), Anjou (see), and Muscadet (see). The best wines from the eastern and westernmost areas are very dry. From the middle areas—Anjou and Touraine—the best wines are lusciously sweet. The major white grape varieties: in the Lower Loire, Sauvignon Blanc; in Anjou and Touraine, Chenin Blanc; in the Upper Loire, Muscadet.

According to legend, it was in the Loire in about the year 345 that the practice of pruning the vine originated. And in a most curious fashion. Saint Martin is credited with the discovery, but it seems that it was actually a much more humble being at whose feet—all four of them—the credit should be laid. It was none other than Saint Martin's ass. Saint Martin had left the animal tethered at the end of a row of vines while he spoke with the monks who tended the vineyard. When he returned, he discovered to his chagrin that the beast had munched on the tender young leaves and shoots of a number of vines chomping them right down to the stalks. The vines were given up for lost. But in the fall, much to the amazement of the monks and Saint Martin himself, those vines bore the finest fruit. From that time, the monks began systematically pruning the vines and the practice spread throughout the region, and beyond.

Loudenne, Château, Fr. A pleasant white wine produced in the Médoc region of Bordeaux. It is similar to a good Graves (see).

Loupiac, Fr. This district opposite Barsac on the east bank of the Garonne River, although part of the Premières Côtes de Bordeaux, has its own controlled appellation of origin (AC). The wines of Loupiac are sweet and often heavy, without the class or distinction of the Barsacs. Drink well-chilled, with fruit.

Louvière, Château La, Fr. A pleasant white Graves (see) that offers good value as it is moderately priced.

Lugana, It. A light, dry white wine produced on the western shore of Lake Garda in Lombardy from Trebbiano (see) grapes. The wine tends to be soft, a bit low in acid. It is best within a year of vintage. Drink it with pan-fried fresh-water fish or flounder (sole) meunière. Noted producers: Ambrosi, Pietro Dal Cero, and Girardon.

Lunel See Languedoc.

Lutomer, Yg. The best white wine district of Yugoslavia. This district in Slovenia produces some fair wines from Wälschriesling, Rhine Riesling, Ruländer, Traminer, Sylvaner, and Pinot Blanc grapes. The Rhine Riesling has the best reputation. Serve with spicy seafood, poultry, or veal dishes.

Luxembourg Luxembourg lies across the river from the Upper Mosel district of Germany and produces similar wines but of less distinction. Generally, the wines of

Luxembourg are white, light-bodied, low in alcohol, and with a refreshing acidity. Unlike the German wines, though, they tend toward the drier end of the scale. They are best, as a rule, drunk young. The most common grape varieties: Auxerrois, Elbling, Pinot Blanc, Pinot Gris, Riesling, Rivaner, Sylvaner, and Traminer. Luxembourg wines usually carry a geographical name and a grape name. The better wines will also carry a vineyard name and a vintage date. Some of the more highly regarded towns: Ahn, Bech-Kleinmacher, Ehnen, Greveldange, Grevenmacher, Lenningen, Machtum, Mertert, Remerschen, Stadtbredimus, Wasserbillig, Wellenstein, and Wormeldange. Generally these wines go very well with fresh-water fish, pan-fried, broiled, or poached, or flounder (sole). These wines offer fine value.

Mâcon, Fr. One of the major wine-producing regions of Burgundy, south of the Côte Chalonnaise and north of Beaujolais. The Mâcon is primarily a white wine region. The wines of Mâcon are generally light to medium in body, dry, firm, and balanced. In dryness, they are in between Chablis and the Côte de Beaune whites. In price, they are among the world's bargains, particularly those labeled Mâcon, Pinot-Chardonnay-Mâcon, Mâcon Supérieur, or Mâcon Villages. Mâcon Supérieur is more frequently used for red wines; Mâcon Villages is always white. Most wines labeled simply Mâcon Blanc or Pinot-Chardonnay-Mâcon are from the northern areas. The Mâcon Villages are in the central part of the region. A wine labeled simply

Mâcon Villages without a village name is most likely a blend of wines from one or more of the following villages: Chardonnay, Clessé, Lugny, and Viré. Wines entirely from one of these villages will more than likely carry the village name. If the wine is from a premier cru vineyard within one of those villages, it will probably carry the vineyard name as well. For example, Mâcon Lugny Les Charmes is a Mâcon Blanc from the Charmes vineyard of Lugny. The most highly regarded Mâcon wines are from the southern section: Pouilly-Fuissé, Pouilly-Loché, Pouilly-Vinzelles, and St.-Véran (see individual listings). These wines are always more expensive but not always better than the Mâcon Villages wines. The Mâcon wines are dry wines that go well with roast veal, poultry, or fish. Mâcon is a food wine par excellence. Bouchard, Drouhin, and Jadot are good producers of Mâcon wines.

Mâconnais See Mâcon.

Mai Wein See May Wine.

Malartic-Lagravière, Château, Fr. One of the better white Graves (see).

Malle, Château de, Fr. A second-growth Sauternes (see).

Malvasia Originally from Greece, this ancient vine grows profusely throughout the Mediterranean area. It is heavily planted in southern Italy, where it produces a number of dessert wines, some fortified, some not, all sweet. It is also grown in central and northern Italy, France, Spain, California, and many other countries. But it produces its best wines in southern Italy. In France it is also known as Malvoisie. (See individual listings.)

Malvasia Bianca, U.S. A fortified aperitif or dessert wine produced in California. Beringer 'makes a good one.

Malvasia di Bosa, It. A Sardinian dessert (dolce naturale) or aperitif wine (secco) from the Malvasia grape. It is made in two types: dry (secco) and sweet (dolce), both rather high in alcohol. Both are also available in fortified versions (liquoroso). All are full-bodied, flavorful, and have a slightly bitter aftertaste.

Malvasia di Cagliari, It. This Sardinian Malvasia, produced in the province of Cagliari, is quite similar to Malvasia di Bosa (see).

Malvasia di Sardegna, It. A Sardinian Malvasia quite similar to Malvasia di Bosa (see).

Malvasia delle Lipari, It. A white wine produced from Malvasia grapes on the Aeolian or Lipari islands off Sicily. There are three versions. All have a full, fruity, Muscat-like aroma, are full-flavored, fruity, and sweet. These wines are best after dinner with fresh fruit or nuts. The regular type is often the least sweet and certainly the lowest in alcohol. The Passito Malvasia della Lipari, from dried grapes, is high in alcohol and very sweet. The fortified Liquoroso is also very sweet and high in alcohol.

Malvazija Istarska, Yg. A Yugoslavian wine from the Malvasia (see) grape made in the Istrian Peninsula.

Malvoisie, Fr. The French name for Malvasia (see).

Malvoisie, Sw. The Swiss name for the Pinot Gris (see).

Malvoisie de Nus, It. A Malvasia wine produced in the Val d'Aosta region of Italy from a variety of Pinot grapes. Don Augusto Pramotton (Cure de Nus) is a good producer.

Mantonico See Montonico.

Manzanilla, Sp. The driest of the Sherries. It is fortified, but only lightly. This wine is high in alcohol (15-16%), bone dry, and has a salty tang. Some claim this comes from the sea winds which blow over the vineyards of Sanlúcar de Barrameda. It is at its best when freshly bottled, and doesn't keep long despite the high alcohol. Manzanilla makes a fine aperitif—one of the best. It also goes well with hors d'oeuvres—shrimp, olives, mussels. La Guita ("the string") is one of the best, if not the best, available.

Margaux, Pavillon Blanc de Château See Pavillon Blanc de Château Margaux.

Marino, It. One of the better-known Castelli Romani wines (see). It is best when very young and fresh. The Marino seen in this country is already too old. This wine tends to be bland and neutral with low acidity. Serve well-chilled, with spicy poultry or fish dishes.

Martina or **Martina Franca, It.** A rather coarse, common wine produced in the southern Italian region of Apulia and often shipped north to be used in the production of Vermouth. It has very little to recommend it. Giuseppe Strippoli is perhaps the most highly regarded producer.

Martini, Louis M., U.S. This Napa Valley winery produces a respectable Gewurztraminer. It also produces a Folle Blanche.

Maryland, U.S. See Boordy Vineyards and Montbray Wine Cellars.

Masson, Paul, U.S. A California winery that produces a pleasant Emerald Riesling (see) under the name Emerald Dry.

Maximin Grünhaus(er), Gm. Maximin Grünhaus is one of the two finest wine towns of the Ruwer (see), and perhaps the most famous. These wines, at their best, are light and delicate with an enchanting flowery perfume. The 120 acres are mostly planted to Riesling. Some Müller-Thurgau is also planted here, but very little. C. von Schubert is by far the most important producer, owning nearly half of the vineyards of this village. Maximin Grünhauser vineyards: Bruderberg, Herrenberg, Abtsberg. Grosslage (general site): Römerlay.

Mayacamas Vineyards, U.S. A California winery which produces a fine Chardonnay that is full and rich.

May Wine, Gm. A German wine flavored with woodruff. It is light, semisweet, and has an herby aroma and flavor of woodruff. Traditionally, this wine is drunk in May with strawberries and perhaps other fruits floating in the glass—the Mai Bowle (May Bowl). The May Wines in this country are never as good as those in Germany. Poor imitations are made here using native American grape varieties.

Melnik, Cz. A noted wine town in Czechoslovakia producing what some claim are the best white wines of that country.

Melon de Bourgogne, Fr. Another name for the Muscadet (see) grape.

Mercurey, Fr. One of the best-known wine towns of the Côte Chalonnaise (see), producing mostly red wines. But some very good white Burgundies from the Chardonnay grape are also produced here. The white Mercureys are a good accompaniment to roast pork or veal. Emile Voarick is one of the most noted producers.

Meursault, Fr. The biggest white wine town of the Côte de Beaune in Burgundy. Meursault produces about 40% of all the white wine from the Côte de Beaune. The only village in this area producing more wine is Pommard, and it is all red. The name Meursault is said to come from the Latin, *Muris Saltus,* meaning "mouse jump." It was said that the vineyards for red and white wines here were only a mouse jump apart. Now, practically all the wine of Meursault is white. The wines of Meursault are the most consistent of the major white wine towns. And they are the least expensive; there are no grand cru vineyards in Meursault to illuminate the lesser wines of the village. The wines of Meursault are primarily from the Chardonnay grape; some Pinot Blanc is also grown. These wines are generally pale straw in color with a bouquet reminiscent of wheat— some say hazelnuts, others oatmeal. On the palate they are dry, though less so than the wines of Puligny and Chassagne-Montrachet to the south; they have an underlying softness. They are full-bodied, and flavorful; the flavor has been described as like ripe, or overripe, peaches. Meursault is a fine wine to accompany roast pork or veal; it goes well with roast poultry as well. The best Meursault vineyards: Les Charmes, Les Genevrières, La Goutte d'Or, and Les Perrières. Other premier crus: Les Bouchères, Les Cras, Les Caillerets, Les Petures, Le Porusot, Le Porusot-Dessus, Les Santenots-Blancs, and Les Santenots-du-Milieu. The premier cru vineyards of Blagny-La Jennelotte, La Pièce-sous-le-Bois, and Sous le Dos d'Ane are usually sold as Meursault (see Blagny). Comtes Lafon, Leroy, and Jacques Prieur produce some outstanding Meursaults.

Louis Latour, Ropiteau, and Prosper Maufoux are other reliable producers.

Mexico   Like those of most countries in the temperate zone, the white wines of Mexico are common, neutral, low in acid, and lacking distinction. There are some signs that technology is improving some of Mexico's white wines, but at present no whites of consequence are seen in this country.

Mirassou Vineyards, U.S.   A Santa Clara-based winery producing some good whites, notably Chenin Blanc, Monterey Riesling (not a true Riesling, but a Sylvaner), Gewurztraminer (often among California's best), and Fleuri Blanc (a dessert wine from Gewurztraminer and other varieties).

Mis en Bouteilles au Château, Fr.   Estate bottled.

Mis en Bouteilles au Domaine, Fr.   Estate bottled.

Missouri Riesling   A native American grape variety with a pervasive grapey aroma and taste. No similarity to the Riesling at all.

Mittelrhein, Gm.   The northernmost wine region (Anbaugebiete) of Germany. In terms of vineyard area, only the Hessische Bergstrasse and Ahr are smaller. The Mittelrhein, in the northwestern corner of Germany's viticultural area, is planted nearly 80% to Riesling and almost 12% to Müller-Thurgau. Bacharach, Bacharach-Steeg, Boppard, Kaub, Oberdiebach, and Oberwesel are the most important wine towns.

Moelleux, Fr.   Mellow—full of body and flavor. This term is used to describe the sweeter Chenin Blancs (see), such as Vouvray and Quarts de Chaume (see), from the Loire Valley (see also Anjou and Touraine).

Monbazillac, Fr. A sweet, rich dessert wine from the Dordogne. It is similar to, but softer and with less distinction than the Sauternes. It is also less expensive. Monbazillac goes well with ripe fruit or fruit salad.

Mondavi Winery, Robert, U.S. A Napa Valley-based winery which makes a good Fumé Blanc (Sauvignon Blanc).

Monsupello, It. A white wine from a blend of Riesling Renano and Riesling Italico grapes produced by Carlo Boatti in Pavia.

Montagny, Fr. One of the two most important white wine towns of the Côte Chalonnaise (see). Louis Latour produces a very fine Montagny.

Montbray Wine Cellars, U.S. A winery in Maryland producing wines from European grape varieties. Notable whites: Chardonnay, White Riesling, and Muscat Ottonel.

Montecarlo, It. A Tuscan wine made from Trebbiano, Sémillon, Pinot Gris, Pinot Bianco, Vermentino, Sauvignon, and Roussanne grapes. This last variety is one of the white varieties used in white Hermitage (see). The Montecarlo can be interesting, but is not often seen outside of Tuscany. It is best when young, within a year of the vintage, as it doesn't live long. Montecarlo is light and balanced with sufficient acid. As it tends to be somewhat delicate, it is a good choice for simply prepared fresh-water fish or roast chicken.

Montecompatri See Montecompatri-Colonna

Montecompatri-Colonna, It. This white wine is produced a few miles south of Rome from Malvasia, Trebbiano, and other grape varieties. Generally light to medium in body, low in acid, off-dry to semi-sweet and rather neutral in character. Drink very young. It tends to be very similar to most of the other white wines of this area (see Castelli Romani, Frascati, Marino, Velletri).

Montée de Tonnerre, Fr. A first-growth (premier cru) Chablis (see).

Monterey Riesling   See Mirassou Vineyards.

Monterey Vineyard, U.S.   A Mont rey County winery producing a couple of good whites: Del Mar Ranch and Gruner Sylvaner.

Monterosso Val d'Arda, It.   A white wine produced in Emilia-Romagna from Malvasia, Moscato, Trebbiano, and other varieties. It is off-dry to semi-sweet, low in alcohol, and fruity. Monterosso Val d'Arda is best when very young. It can be pleasant, but no more.

Monteviña, U.S.   An Amador County winery producing perhaps the best white Zinfandel in California.

Monthélie, Fr.   A village in the Côte de Beaune producing some white wine that is often fine value.

Montilla, Sp.   These wines, made from the Pedro Ximénez grape around Córdoba in Spain, resemble Sherry and are made in a similar way. The grapes ripen to such an extent that these wines have quite a high natural alcohol: 15%, 16%, or more. After fermentation, as in Sherry, a yeast known as Flor forms on the surface of the wine and imparts a unique aroma and flavor. The wine is aged above ground in ventilated bodegas. All Montilla is the result of a fractional blending (Solera) system; the younger wines are added to the older wines to take on their complexities. In its most simplified form, assuming a Solera of three tiers, some wine from the oldest tier, usually less than one-quarter of the barrel, is drawn out for bottling. The barrel is then filled up with the next-to-oldest wine. These barrels in turn are filled up with the youngest of the three wines. The youngest tier is then topped up with the new wine. The Solera date is the year the Solera was begun. Theoretically there is some wine from that date in the wine. But this is not just a blend; the older wine "educates" the younger wine by mellowing it and adding character. The younger wine refreshes the older wine. The biggest differences between Sherry and Montilla: Sherry is produced about 100 miles south of Montilla; the predominant grape variety in Sherry is Palomino, in Montilla, Pedro Ximénez; Sherry is fortified, Montilla is usually not. Montilla is made in a variety of styles. From the lightest and driest to the fullest and sweetest: Fino, Amontillado, Oloroso, Cream, Pedro Ximénez. A well-chilled Fino is a perfect aperitif by itself or with *tapas* (hors d'oeuvres) or shellfish. Amontillado goes well with soups or spicy chicken dishes; Oloroso, with cheeses; Cream Montillas with cakes; Pedro Ximénez, dark, full, rich, sweet, and thick, is best sipped like a liqueur, or with nuts. Alvear and Montialbero (Spanish Gold) are two very fine producers.

Montlouis, Fr. This Loire Valley wine is produced around the village of Montlouis near Vouvray in Touraine. It is very similar to Vouvray (see), but because it is not so well known it is usually very fine value. And the quality is not significantly less than that of Vouvray. Best when young. Drink the drier Montlouis with poultry or fish in cream sauces; the sweeter style with fruit.

Montonaco   See Montonico.

Montonico, It.   This grape, grown in Calabria in the "toe" of the Italian "boot," produces a big, fruity, aromatic wine with an aroma and flavor of apricots. It is often fortified and can be sweet or semi-sweet. Definitely a desert wine; it goes well with fruit or nuts. Umberto Ceratti and Calabro Ionica Bianchese are respected producers.

Montrachet, Fr.   By reputation, the greatest single dry white wine vineyard of the world. Unfortunately it doesn't always live up to its reputation, though judging by the price, that would be difficult to tell. At its best there aren't enough superlatives to describe this wine. The 19-acre Montrachet vineyard is divided between Chassagne and Puligny. These two towns append the name of their most famous vineyard to their own names. The name Montrachet is reputedly from the Latin, *Mons Rachicensis,* "Bald Hill," and the top of the Montrachet hill is indeed quite bare. Le Montrachet vineyard is in the center of the hill, Chevalier-Montrachet (nearly 18 acres) is above, Bâtard-Montrachet (29½ acres), below. Portions of Bâtard-Montrachet and Montrachet itself are in both villages of Puligny and Chassagne-Montrachet. Bienvenue-Bâtard-Montrachet (9½ acres) is on the Puligny-Montrachet side of Bâtard-Montrachet; Criots-Bâtard-Montrachet (3½ acres) is on the Chassagne side. These vineyards are labeled individually. Le Montrachet is known for its power and authority, its balance and breed. This wine has been described as perfection itself. At its best Montrachet is full, rich, and fruity, dry yet seemingly sweet, smooth-textured yet firm. The largest producers of Montrachet (not necessarily the best): Bouchard Père et Fils, Marquis de Laguiche, and Baron Thénard. The Montrachet of the Domaine de la Romanée-Conti is nothing short of extraordinary. Jacques Prieur is also a good name to look for.

Montravel, Fr. This wine from the Dordogne valley in southeastern France is made in a few styles, ranging from off-dry to semi-sweet. When drunk young and fresh, the off-dry style can be quite good with cream chicken dishes. Drink the semi-sweet with fruit. Montravel is often a fine value. Look for Louis Dubroca.

Monts-de-Milieu, Fr. A premier cru (first-growth) Chablis (see).

Moore's Diamond See Diamond.

Mór, Hn. A district of Hungary producing some fair to good white wine from the Ezerjo grape, labeled Móri Ezerjó.

Morey-St.-Denis, Fr. This well-known Burgundian village produces mostly red wines. But some white wine is produced in the premier cru vineyard of Monts-Luisants.

Morio Muskat This German hybrid variety is a cross between Sylvaner and Weissburgunder. Most of the Morio Muskat is planted in the Rheinpfalz (Palatinate) and Rheinhessen; some is also grown in Baden. These wines are full, off-dry to sweet, and have a slight Muscat aroma.

Moscatel Portuguese and Spanish for Muscat (see).

Moscatel de Setúbal, Pr. One of the finest fortified Muscat dessert wines of the world. This Portuguese wine challenges Italy's best. Moscatel de Setúbal is amber-colored, fragrant, full-bodied, sweet, and rich. Sip alone, or drink with fruit or nuts.

Moscato   See Muscat.

Moscato di Cagliari, It.   A Muscat dessert wine from the province of Cagliari in Sardinia. It is made as Dolce Naturale (sweet natural) and Liquoroso Dolce Naturale (fortified sweet natural). Drink after dinner with fruit and cakes.

Moscato di Noto, It.   A Sicilian dessert wine from Muscat grapes, made in regular and fortified (Liquoroso) styles. Both are sweet with a fragrant Muscat aroma. Drink with fresh fruit or not-too-sweet cakes.

Moscato di Pantelleria, It.   This Sicilian dessert wine is made from Zibibbo grapes. The Naturale (natural) is the lowest in alcohol, next is the Vino Naturalmente Dolce (naturally sweet wine), then the Liquoroso (fortified). A regular and fortified Passito are made from overripe grapes left to hang on the vine after the normal harvest and dry almost to raisins. All are quite sweet, with a fragrant Muscat aroma and flavor. Drink with fruit, cakes, and other desserts. F. Maccotta is a highly respected producer.

Moscato di Siracusa, It.   A dessert wine from Sicily made from the Muscat grape.

Moscato di Sorso-Sennori, It.   A dessert wine from the Muscat grape made in Sardinia. As is typical, the wine is made in unfortified and fortified (Liquoroso) types.

Moscato di Trani, It.   A dessert wine made from Muscat grapes in Apulia, in the "heel" of Italy. It is golden in color with an aroma of ripe fruit, full-flavored, and sweet. It is rather pleasant, especially when drunk with stoned fruits (apricots, peaches, nectarines), mixed fruit, or berries. The Dolce Naturale (sweet natural) is about 13% alcohol; the fortified (Liquoroso) reaches at least 16%. Felice Botta is a very fine producer.

Mosel-Saar-Ruwer, Gm. One of the eleven wine-producing regions (Anbaugebiete) of Germany comprising nearly 30,000 acres. The Mosel wines at their best are the lightest and most refreshing of Germany, with an extraordinary balance of fruit and acid. They are known for their fragrant, flowery perfume and their delicacy. The best wines come from the Mittel (Middle) Mosel from Mehring to Enkirch, the Saar (see), and the Ruwer (see). The Bereich (subregion) of Bernkastel encompasses the towns from Briedel to Kenn—more of an extension than from Enkirch to Mehring. There is disagreement among experts over the actual extent of the Middle Mosel. The only thing agreed upon are the best villages: Piesport, Bernkastel, Wehlen, Graach, Zeltingen, Brauneberg, Erden, and Urzig (see individual listings). The river in this area flows in loops and turns. The distance from Mehring to Enkirch in a straight line is only about 15 miles; by car, it is nearly tripled (40 miles). The best vineyards face south and are planted on very steep slopes on slate hillsides. The Grosslagen (general sites) for Bereich (subregion) Bernkastel: Badstube, Beerenlay, Kurfürstlay, Michelsberg, Münzlay, Nacktarsch, Probstberg, St. Michael, Schwarzlay, and Vom Heissen Stein. Of the major grape varieties in the Mosel-Saar-Ruwer, Riesling accounts for nearly 66%, Müller-Thurgau just under 20%, and Elbling 10%. Most of the Elbling is grown in the Upper Mosel. The Riesling is by far the most widely planted grape variety in the Middle Mosel. Among the most important producers: Adams-Bergweiler, Zach. Bergweiler-Prüm Erben, Bischöfliches Konvikt, Bischöfliches Priesterseminar, Dr. Deinhard, Friedrich Wilhelm Gymnasium, Kath. Pfarrkirche St. Michael, Reichsgraf von Kesselstatt, Licht-Bergweiler, Franz Josef Liell, Dr. Melsheimer, Pauly-Bergweiler, Joh. Jos. Prüm, Peter Prüm, Sebastian Alois Prüm, St. Nikolaus Hospital, Freiherr von Schorlemer, Dr. H. Thanisch, and Vereinigte Hospitien.

Moselblümchen, Gm. "Little flower of the Mosel," one of the most popular German wines sold in the United States. But not one of the best. Moselblümchen is a shippers' wine, usually a blend of the cheapest wines. It is often sold for more than its quality warrants. This is not the counterpart on the Mosel to the Rhines' Liebfraumilch (see); its average quality is considerably lower.

Moselle See Mosel.

Moselle, U.S. At least one California producer bottles a wine labeled "Moselle." The name evokes the charm of that fine German wine region, but the wine does not.

Müller-Thurgau This hybrid grape was thought to be a Riesling and Sylvaner cross, but is now believed to be a cross between two Riesling vines. Generally the Müller-Thurgau wines are light, soft, and fast-maturing. They lack the elegant balance and distinction of the Rieslings. The Müller-Thurgau wines are often good, and being less expensive than the Rieslings, are also good value. Müller-Thurgau is the most widely planted variety in Germany. In percentages by region: the Ahr is 19% Müller-Thurgau; Mosel-Saar-Ruwer, 19%; Mittelrhein, 12%; Rheingau, 11%; Nahe, 31%; Rheinhessen, 36%; Palatinate (Rheinpfalz), 24%; Hessische Bergstrasse, 20%; Franconia, 45%; Württemberg, 10%; and Baden, 33%. Müller-Thurgau is also grown in northern Italy, where it is sometimes labeled Riesling X Sylvaner, in Austria, central Europe, and England. In fact, some quite respectable Müller-Thurgau wines have been produced in England, though very little, and they are almost never seen here. There are also plantings in New Zealand. In Alsace it is a secondary variety and, in fact, produces rather undistinguished wines, which is surprising as both the Riesling and Sylvaner do quite well there. In Yugoslavià Müller-Thurgau is known as Rizvanac Bijeli.

Some good Müller-Thurgaus are produced in Italy: Motelio, Faravelli, and Isimbarda in Pavia; Monterotondo Gavi from Maria Fugazza Busch in the Piedmont; Schiopetto in Gorizia, Deroà in Treviso, Molinelli in Piacenza, and Abbazia Novacella in Bolzano produce good Italian whites from the Müller-Thurgau grape.

Murfatlar, Rm. A Rumanian dessert wine made from the Muskat Ottonel grape.

Muscadet, Fr. If any wine can challenge the dryness of Chablis, that wine is Muscadet. Muscadet is a pale-colored, light-bodied wine with very little aroma, and it is bone dry. Muscadet is produced around Nantes, in

Brittany, along the lower Loire, from the Muscadet, or Melon de Bourgogne, grape. A second grape, Gros Plant (see Folle Blanche), is also planted here, but the wines made from it are not as good as the Muscadets. Muscadet is produced in two major zones, Sèvre-et-Maine and the Coteaux de la Loire. The better wines are reputedly from the former. Wine labeled simply Muscadet may be a blend of wines from both regions, or else a wine from neither. This wine is generally not as highly regarded as the Muscadet from those two regions. But it depends on the producer—Château de la Bidière, Marquis de Goulaine and Domaine de l'Hyvernière are among the best, yet are only labeled Muscadet-sur-Lie. Sur Lie ("on the lees") means that the wine was bottled in March following the vintage without having been racked (drawn off the lees). This makes a fresher wine. The Sur Lie wine is best within the year. In fact, all Muscadet is best very young, while it retains its youthful freshness. Served well-chilled, its refreshing acidity makes this a thirst-quenching wine. Only Chablis and Manzanilla go so well with oysters as Muscadet.

Muscadine A species of native American grapes which grow in the southeastern states. The technical name for the species is *Vitis rotundifolia.* Scuppernong (see) is the best-known variety. These wines are an acquired taste.

Muscat Muscat grape varieties are grown in almost all wine-producing countries. Muscat is used most often to produce sweet, rich dessert wines, sometimes fortified—especially in the southern regions (southern Italy, Spain, Portugal, and southern France). The most highly regarded Muscat varieties are Frontignan or Canelli, and Ottonel. Related varieties and other names for the Muscat: Aleatico, Moscadelle, Moscato (see), Muskat, Muskateller (see), Moscatello, Moscadelle, Moscatel (see), and Muscatel. Some of the best French Muscats are from Beaumes de Venise (see), Frontignan (see), Lunel (see Languedoc), and Rivesaltes (see). California and northern Italy produce some light-bodied, sweet Muscats that are low in alcohol and have a slight sparkle. Angelo Papagni's Moscato d'Angelo and Louis Martini's Moscato Amabile are fine examples from California. These are wines to be drunk alone or with ripe fruit.

Muscat Alexandria, U.S. The Angelo Papagni Winery of California produces a good Muscat Alexandria. It is aromatic, off-dry, full-bodied, well-balanced, and fruity. A good choice with spicy fish or poultry dishes, including curries.

Muscat Blanc See Muscat.

Muscat d'Alsace, Fr. There seems to be some disagreement over whether or not this grape is actually a Muscat. The Muscat d'Alsace wines from the Alsatian towns of Ribeauvillé, Riquewihr, and Voegtlinshoffen are highly regarded.

Muscat de Frontignan This grape variety, named for the town of Frontignan in France, is actually the same variety as the Muscat di Canelli from the Piedmont in northern Italy. In California, Concannon and the Novitiate of Los Gatos produce good fortified Muscat de Frontignan wines. A fine aperitif or after-dinner drink with nuts.

Muscat Ottonel See Muskat Ottonel.

Muscatel See Muscat.

Musigny, Fr. One of the greatest vineyards of Burgundy. A minuscule amount (about 100 cases) of white is produced from Chardonnay grapes by Comte Georges de Voguë, labeled Musigny Blanc. Its rarity adds to its price, making this one of the most expensive of all the dry white wines. There is more to the price than its scarcity though; this wine has style and breed.

Muskat Ottonel The best wines from this grape variety come from Austria. Dr. Konstantin Frank in New York State produces a very fine, lightly fortified dessert wine from the Muskat Ottonel grape. This variety also grows in Alsace, Germany, Rumania, Yugoslavia, and other Balkan countries.

Muskateller This grape variety, one of the many varieties of the Muscat, is planted in the Baden and Palatinate regions of Germany, as well as the Slovenia region of Yugoslavia and Badacsony region of Hungary as Muskotály.

Muskotály See Muskateller.

Myrat, Château de, Fr. A second-growth Barsac (see).

Nackenheim(er), Gm. The wines of Nackenheim are prized for their remarkable bouquet, elegance, and breed. They are considered the finest wines of the Rheinhessen. At their best they have few equals, and no superiors. Notable producers: Gunderloch-Lange, Gunderloch-Usinger, Louis Guntrum, Heinrich Seip, and Staatlichen Weinbaudomänen. Nackenheimer vineyards: Engelsberg, Rothenberg, and Schmittskapellchen.

Nahe, Gm. One of the eleven recognized German wine
regions (Anbaugebiete), named for the river which
flows through it. The wines of the Nahe are the most
varied of any of the Rhine regions. From an area
between the Mosel and the Rheingau, the wines seem
to take on some of the characteristics of either region,
depending on which region is closer. Another factor in
the diversity in these wines is the different soils in the
Nahe. The wines from the upper Nahe and the
tributary Glan are more in the style of the Mosel
wines—lighter and more elegant than those from the
rest of the region. The wines from the middle Nahe and
the Alsenz are the fullest of all, tending toward those
from the Palatinate (Rheinpfalz). Those of the lower
Nahe are more refined and more elegant. At one time
the wines of the Nahe were among the most-sought-
after wines of Germany. Now they are not so well
known, but deserve to be better known. These wines
have a fine delicate bouquet and much distinction. And
they are good value. Müller-Thurgau and Sylvaner
comprise nearly 60% of all plantings; Riesling vines
account for slightly under 25%. About 20% of the wine
of the Nahe is made by cooperatives. The leading
towns: Kreuznach, Niederhausen, Norheim, and
Schlossböckelheim (see individual listings). Münster,
Roxheim, and Winzenheim (see) also produce some
good wines. Major producers of the Nahe: August
Anheuser, Rudolf Anheuser, Erbhof Tesch, Carl
Finkenauer, Herf und Engelsmann Erben, Reichsgraf
von Plettenberg, Schlossgut Diel auf Berg Layen, Dr.
Josef Höfer Schlossmühle, Jakob Schneider, Staatlichen
Weinbaudomänen, Staatsweingut Weinbaulehranstalt,

and Weingut Gutleuthof Carl Andres. The Nahe region is divided into two districts (Bereich): Kreuznach and Schloss Böckelheim, named for the two most famous wine towns of the Nahe.

Nairac, Château, Fr.   A second-growth Barsac (see).

Nasco di Cagliari, It.   This Sardinian wine is made from Nasco grapes grown in the province of Cagliari. Generally high in alcohol and low in acid, this wine ranges from off-dry to sweet. A fortified version (Liquoroso) is also made. Better as an aperitif or dessert wine, depending on the version, it goes well with nuts or raisins. The drier versions might accompany spicy and oily fish dishes.

Nederburg, S.A.   A South African vineyard near the Paarl district (see South Africa).

Neuchâtel, Sw.   A Swiss wine-producing region on the northern shore of Lake Neuchâtel. The wines of this region—made from the Chasselas grape—are light and pleasant, dry and tart. They are sometimes slightly pétillant (crackling) and are referred to as star wines. In order to bring out the "stars" (the bubbles), they are poured into the glass from a height. Château d'Auvernier and Ville de Neuchâtel are respected estates. A suitable accompaniment to cheese fondue.

Neumagen(er), Gm.   Neumagen, a wine village on the Mosel, is reputed to be the oldest wine-growing village in Germany. Though not of the highest quality, these wines can be quite good, especially from one of the better producers such as Dünweg, Friedrich Wilhelm Gymnasium, Dr. Ronde, Milz, and Willems'sche Armenstiftung. Neumagener vineyards: Engelgrube,

Goldtröpfchen, Grafenberg, Grosser Hengelberg, Häschen, Hofberger, Laudamusberg, Nusswingert, Rosengärtchen, Roterd, and Sonnenuhr. (See also Dhron.)

New York, U.S. The second-largest wine-producing state in the United States. Wines are produced from native American varieties, French-American hybrids, and European varieties. Those from native American varieties tend to have a pervasive grapey aroma and flavor reminding one of alcoholic grape juice. Before a way was found to combat the phylloxera louse, though, these were the only vines that could be grown in the eastern United States. The wines from the French-American hybrids can be pleasant quaffing wines, especially when young, fresh, and fruity. Some good wines are produced at the Bully Hill (see) estate of Walter Taylor, particularly his Seyval Blanc and Bully Hill White, which are among the best of the French-American hybrid wines. Bully Hill also produces a good Aurora Blanc and Verdelet Blanc. Boordy Vineyards of the Finger Lakes (see) and Ben Marl in the Hudson Valley, among others, also produce wines from French-American hybrids. The best New York State wines are produced from the European varieties: Johannisberg Riesling, Gewurztraminer, and Pinot Chardonnay (see Frank, Dr. Konstantin and Gold Seal). The major wine district of New York State is the Finger Lakes. Wines are also produced in the Hudson River Valley and, of late, on Long Island. There are those who believe that the European varieties will do quite well on Long Island because the weather is not as harsh there as in the Finger Lakes. In that district frosts and freezing winters threaten the vines. But the quality of the Rieslings and Gewurztraminers from the Finger Lakes vineyards makes it worth the struggle against the weather. New York's better wines tend to be austere, with a refreshing acidity; when vinified dry, they are crisp. This makes them good with food. (See also Keuka Lake.)

New Zealand This South Pacific country produces white wine from both the European varieties and the French-American hybrids. Seibel, Rhine Riesling, Müller-Thurgau, Chardonnay, Gewürztraminer, and Chasselas are some of the more common white wine grapes grown in New Zealand. Wines are labeled generically, with the names of European wine regions; varietally, for the grape variety used; and with proprietary names. Very little, if any, white wine from New Zealand is seen in the United States.

Niagara A native American grape variety producing pervasively foxy (grapey) wines, ranging from off-dry to sweet. There is little to recommend it.

Niederhausen(er), Gm. Niederhausen is one of the four best wine-producing towns of the Nahe. These wines are more like those of the Rhine, particularly the Rheinpfalz (Palatinate), than the Mosel. Important producers: August Anheuser, Rudolf Anheuser, von Plettenberg, Jakob Schneider, Staatlichen Weinbaudomänen, and Staatsweingut Weinbaulehranstalt. Niederhäuser vineyards: Felsensteyer, Graukatz, Hermannsberg, Hermannshöhle, Kertz, Klamm, Pfaffenstein, Pfingstweide, Rosenberg, Rosenheck, Steinberg, Steinwingert, and Stollenberg.

Nierstein(er), Gm. The wines from Nierstein are the softest and, some would say, most attractive of the Rheinhessen wines. At their best, they surely challenge the wines of Nackenheim (see). The better Niersteiners have an attractive, fruity perfume and a full, rich flavor. At one time Auflangen, Hipping, and Rehbach were considered the three best vineyards in Nierstein. Today both Niersteiner Rehbach and Niersteiner Auflangen are Grosslage (general site) names—Rehbach now encompassing Brudersberg, Goldene Luft, Hipping, and Pettenthal; and Auflangen taking in Bergkirche, Glöck, Heiligenbaum, Kranzberg, Olberg, Orbel, Schloss Schwabsburg, and Zehnmorgen. Spiegelberg, previously another highly regarded vineyard, is also a Grosslage encompassing Bildstock, Brückchen, Ebersberg, Findling, Hölle, Kirchplatte, Klostergarten, Paterberg, Rosenberg, and Schloss Hohenrechen. None of these sites was previously as highly regarded as Spiegelberg. Pfaffenkappe, in the Gutes Domtal Grosslage, is another recognized Niersteiner vineyard.

The German wine laws were, or so it is claimed, devised to protect the consumer. By turning famous vineyards into Grosslagen it seems they have done just the opposite. Now, the protection the consumer needs is to be protected from the misrepresentations created by the wine laws. In buying Niersteiner wines, it is very important to look for estate-bottled (Erzeuger-Abfüllung) wines from reputable producers such as Anton Balbach Erben, Louis Guntrum, Heinrich Seip Kurfürstenhof, Freiherr Heyl zu Herrnsheim Mathildenhof, Franz Karl Schmitt, Gustav Adolf

Schmitt, Geschwister Schuch, Rheinhold Senfter, Carl Sittmann, Staatlichen Weinbaudomänen, J. u. H. A. Strub, and Vowinkel Erben.

Noah   A native American grape variety producing mediocre wines with a pervasive foxy or grapey aroma and taste.

Norheim(er), Gm.   Norheim is one of the most important wine towns of the Nahe. Norheimer vineyards: Dellchen, Götzenfeld, Kafels, Kirschheck, Klosterberg, Oberberg, Onkelchen, and Sonnenberg.

Novitiate of Los Gatos, U.S.   This California winery makes quite a nice Muscat de Frontignan.

Nuits-Saint-Georges, Fr.   This village in the Côte de Nuits produces mostly red wines, but some white is also made, notably at Clos de l'Arlot (see) and La Perrière, both premier crus (first growths). These wines are similar to the white wines from Aloxe-Corton (see). White Nuits-St.-Georges is a good accompaniment to simple white meats such as roast veal.

Nuragus di Cagliari, It.   This Sardinian wine is made predominantly from Nuragus grapes grown in the province of Cagliari. It is medium-bodied, dry, rather bland, and not very high in alcohol. A wine for seafood in piquant sauces.

Oberemmel(er), Gm.   Oberemmel is one of the better wineproducing towns of the Saar. In great years some of these wines can be truly outstanding. The Oberemmeler wines are light and flowery with the characteristic austerity of Saar wines. In poor years they tend to be hard and acidic. Von Hövel and Reichsgraf von Kesselstatt are important producers. Other good producers: Friedrich Wilhelm Gymnasium, van Wolxem. Oberemmeler vineyards: Agritiusberg, Altenberg, Hütte, Karlsberg, Raul, and Rosenberg. Oberemmel is in the general site (Grosslage) Scharzberg.

Ockfen(er), Gm. When the sun smiles in the Saar, wines from Ockfen can be nothing short of extraordinary—racy wines with few equals. They are known for their outstanding bouquet and their delicacy, so light they seem almost fragile. But they also have that steeliness so common in the Saar wines. The greatest vineyard is Bockstein. Other Ockfener vineyards: Geisberg, Heppenstein, Herrenberg, Kupp, Neuwies, and Zickelgarten. Look for the wines of Dr. Fischer, Friedrich Wilhelm Gymnasium, Gebert, Forstmeister, Geltz Erben, Helmut Gorgen, Max Keller, Adolf Rheinart Erben, Edmund Reverchon, Staatlichen Weinbaudomänen, and Dr. Wagner.

Odobeşti, Rm. Odobeşti is the largest wine-producing area of Rumania. Chasselas, Fetească Albă, Pinot Gris, and Furmint are the grape varieties used in the white wines. Cazacliu, Jaristea, Varsatura, and Virtescoiu are the most important wine-producing villages. The Odobeşti wines are light and dry.

Oeil de Perdrix Literally, "eye of the partridge," describing the color of a white wine made from black-skinned grapes (blanc de noirs). It is actually a very pale bronze or pink-colored wine, the tint picked up from the short contact the juice has with the black skins.

Oesterreicher Another name—literally, Austrian—for the Sylvaner grape (see), especially on the Rheingau.

Oestrich(er), Gm. Oestrich is the largest wine-producing town in the Rheingau, with 750 acres of vines. In terms of quality, these full-bodied wines are second-rate compared to the better Rheingau wines, but being relatively inexpensive, they are often good value. Reputable producers include Mülhens-Berna, Schloss Schönborn, Johann Tillmann Erben, and Geh. Rat Julius Wegeler Erben. Oestricher vineyards: Doosberg, Klosterberg, Lenchen, and Schloss Reichhartshausen. This last vineyard is recognized on its own and need not carry the village name on the label.

Oggau, Au. One of the better wine areas of the Burgenland in Austria.

Olaszrizling See Welschriesling.

Olivier, Château, Fr. A Bordeaux estate producing some fair-quality white Graves (see).

Oltrepò Pavese, It. One of the major wine-producing districts of Lombardy. This controlled denomination of origin (DOC) will be followed by the name of the grape variety the wine was made from: Cortese, Moscato, Pinot (for Pinot Nero and Pinot Grigio), Riesling (Riesling Renano and Riesling Italico are both allowed). The Müller-Thurgau grape is also grown here, but has no legal status under Italian wine law (DOC). Faravelli and Isimbarda produce good Müller-Thurgaus. The Riesling is perhaps the best white wine of Oltrepò Pavese. Generally these white wines are dry (Moscato excepted), tending to be lighter in body than the same varieties grown in Friuli-Venezia-Giulia, and with better acidity. These wines are best when young, perhaps within two years of the vintage. Reliable producers: Balestriere, Denari, Girani, Della Madonna

Isabella, Contessa di San Pietro Rati Opizzoni, dal Pozzo, and Saviotti.

Ontario A native American grape variety which produces mediocre wines with an excessive grapiness.

Oppenheim(er), Gm. Oppenheim is one of the most important wine-producing towns of the Rheinhessen (see). The wines, while not as good as those from Nierstein (see), can be and often are quite good—soft, full-bodied, fruity, and with charm. The wines of Oppenheim, like most of those from Hessia, are rather fast-maturing. Important producers: Dr. Dahlem Erben, Geschwister Schuch, Louis Guntrum, Jungkenn Erben, Carl Koch Erben, Landes-Lehr-und Versuchanstalt, Carl Sittmann, Gustav Adolf Schmitt, Staatlichen Weinbaudomänen Mainz, Staatsweingut Oppenheim, and Weingut der Stadt Oppenheim. Oppenheimer vineyards: Daubhaus, Gutleuthaus, Herrenberg, Herrengarten, Kreuz, Paterhof, Sackträger, Schloss, Schlossberg, Schützenhütte, and Zuckerberg.

Optima A hybrid grape produced from a Sylvaner X Riesling X Müller-Thurgau cross.

Ortega A hybrid grape from a Müller-Thurgau X Siegerrebe cross, producing full-bodied, fruity wines.

Ortsteil, Gm. A vineyard whose name on the label is not required to be qualified by the village name, for example, Steinberger, Scharzhofberger, Schloss Vollrads, Schloss Johannisberger.

Orvieto, It. A rather mediocre wine made from Trebbiano and other varieties grown in Umbria. The wine is named for the medieval town of Orvieto. These wines range from off-dry (secco) to semi-sweet (abboccato).

The abboccato is generally better, as the sugar masks poor pasteurization which gives the wines a somewhat cooked aroma and flavor. Generally overpriced for its quality. Best drunk as young as possible. Like many Italian whites, Orvieto has a slightly bitter aftertaste which increases with age.

Paarl, S.A.   One of the best wine regions of South Africa (see).

Pagadebit di Bertinoro, It.   A white wine from Pagadebit grapes produced in Emilia-Romagna by Mario Pezzi.

Paille, Vin de, Fr.   "Straw wine"—a white wine made from grapes that have been dried on straw mats until they are practically raisins. This wine is golden, sweet, rich, and high in alcohol. The best Vin de Paille of France is produced in Hermitage (Chave makes one in small amounts) and the Jura. (See also Passito.) These wines are, of course, dessert wines, suitable for drinking with nuts, perhaps fruit, or by themselves.

Palatinate, Gm.   The Palatinate, or Rheinpfalz, is the largest wine-producing region of Germany, responsible for approximately one-fifth of its total wine production. This region covers over 51,000 acres. It is bordered by the Rhein on the east, France on the south and southwest, the Saar region on the west, and the Rheinhessen to the north. The Palatinate has the warmest and driest weather of all the German regions. Germany's most famous wine route—the Deutsche Weinstrasse—runs through the Palatinate, beginning at the Weintor (wine gate) of Schweigen on the French border, and continuing for about 50 miles to Klein-bockenheim on the Hessian border. The Palatinate is divided into two subregions (Bereich): Südliche Weinstrasse, in the south, extending from Neustadt south; and the Mittelhaardt-Deutsche Weinstrasse, in the 'north, from Neustadt to the Hessian border. Prior to the new wine laws (1971), experts divided the Palatinate into three subregions: the Unter- (lower) Haardt, in the south, the Mittel- (middle) Haardt, and Ober- (upper) Haardt, in the north. The best section, the Mittel-Haardt, covered the seventeen villages in the area from Herxheim to Neustadt. Including those villages north of Herxheim in the Bereich Mittelhaardt Deutsche Weinstrasse did nothing to improve the quality of those wines. The best villages, all in the middle section, are from north to south: Wachenheim, Forst, Deidesheim, and Ruppertsberg (see individual listings). One rung below these four are Kallstadt, Ungstein, Bad Dürkheim, and Königsbach (see Dürkheim, Kallstadt, and Königsbach). The major grape varieties of the Rheinpfalz: Sylvaner (33%), Müller-Thurgau (23%), Riesling (14%). The best wines, as elsewhere in Germany, are from the Riesling. If the label doesn't say Riesling the wine is probably not from that noble variety. About 40% of the Pfalz wine is produced by cooperatives. The three most important producers, referred to as "the three B's," are Geh. Rat Dr. von Bassermann-Jordan, Reichsrat von Buhl, and Dr. Bürklin-Wolf. All have major holdings in the best villages. Other important producers: Dr. Deinhard, Wilhelm Spindler, Hch. Koch-Herzog Erben, Dr. Jos. Pioth, Stumpf-Fitz'sches Weingut Annaberg, Georg Siben Erben, Josef Biffar, Dietz-Matti, Herbert Giessen

Erben, Heinrich Spindler, Eugen Spindler-Weingut Lindenhof, Weingut Hahnhof, K. Fitz-Ritter, Carl Josef Hoch, H. Karst. The wines of the Palatinate are fuller in body and flavor than the other Rhein wines; they are also softer and more mellow, having lower acidity, but they are well-balanced. Coming from the mildest wine region, these wines are more consistent from year to year, but that doesn't mean that every year is equal in quality. There are bad years here as well as elsewhere in Germany. The wines of the Palatinate go better with food than those of the Mosel or Rheingau because they are less delicate, fuller. Drink with poultry, fresh-water fish, or simple veal dishes (such as wienerschnitzel).

Palette, Fr.   A white wine produced near Aix-en-Provence. A good wine to accompany bouillabaisse or seafood in piquant sauces.

Papagni Winery, Angelo, U.S.   A California winery which produces a fine Muscat Alexandria and a light Muscat labeled Moscato d'Angelo. Its Chenin Blanc is also quite agreeable. Angelo Papagni also produces some good Emerald Rieslings.

Parducci Wine Cellars, U.S.   A Mendocino-based California winery that produces a very good French Colombard and Chenin Blanc.

Parnay, Château de, Fr.   A noted estate in the Saumur (see) district of the Loire Valley.

Parrina Bianco, It.   A white wine from Tuscany made from Trebbiano, Malvasia, and other varieties. It is generally common and undistinguished, with low acid and a trace of bitterness at the end. Drink within a year of the vintage; it can be pleasant when young enough.

Passito, It. Describes a wine made from overripe, dried ("passa") grapes. Often used as an additional qualifier on Moscato and Malvasia dessert wines. These wines are high in alcohol and can be either sweet or semisweet. (See also Caluso Passito and Paille, Vin de.)

Passito di Chambave, It. A very rare dessert wine. It is produced by Ezio Voyat from Muscat grapes grown high up in the Val d'Aosta. It is very highly esteemed, but unfortunately seldom seen outside Italy. (See Passito.)

Patras, Gc. Fortified white wines produced near Athens.

Patrimonio, Fr. One of the better-known white wines of Corsica. It is coarse, full-bodied, low in acid, and high in alcohol. Drink cold, with spicy seafood dishes or poultry in piquant sauces.

Pavillon Blanc de Château Margaux, Fr. A white wine produced by the highly regarded red-wine estate, Château Margaux, in the Haut-Médoc area of Burgundy (see).

Pedroncelli Winery, U.S. A California winery in the Dry Creek Valley of Sonoma which produces a reasonably priced Gewurztraminer.

Perelada, Sp. A rather neutral and undistinguished white wine named for the town of production in the Spanish Pyrenees.

Perle A hybrid grape variety, from a Gewürztraminer and Müller-Thurgau cross, grown in Germany.

Pernand-Vergelesses, Fr. One of the least-known villages in

Burgundy. Much of this wine is sold as Corton-Charlemagne (see). What little white wine there is that is labeled Pernand-Vergelesses can be quite inexpensive, and therefore very fine value. A good wine with veal, poultry, or fish. (See Aloxe-Corton.)

Peru Very little, if any, white wine from Peru is imported into this country. It tends to have been left too long in wood for the American palate.

Petit Chablis See Chablis.

Phelps Vineyard, Joseph, U.S. A Napa Valley vineyard which has produced the most exciting Johannisberg Riesling to thus far come out of California—notably its 1976 and 1975 Special Selection Late Harvest wines, particularly the 1976. Both are thick, luscious dessert wines, the 1976 more so.

Piave, or **Vini del Piave,** It. An area in Veneto covering parts of the provinces of Treviso and Venezia. The white varieties allowed for this controlled denomination of origin (DOC) are Tocai and Verduzzo. The Tocai is similar to those of Friuli-Venezia-Giulia (see). The Verduzzo is the more interesting of the two wines. Both wines are best within a year of the vintage and too often those seen in the United States are too old, having lost their fruit and gone flat. They are generally low in acid and have a slightly bitter finish which becomes more pronounced with age. Bianchi Kunkler produces a very good Pinot Gris in this area. It is not a DOC wine. Italian wine law doesn't recognize this variety for the Piave River DOC. When very young, it is one of the best white wines of the area. Drink with fresh-water fish or poultry.

Picolit, It. A very rare Italian dessert wine produced from Picolit grapes in the Colli Orientali del Friuli area of Friuli-Venezia-Giulia. It has been called "the Château d'Yquem of Italy," and in one respect the comparison is valid: price. Picolit is very expensive. In fact, it is overpriced. This is because of its rarity. This wine is full-bodied, yet delicate, sweet, and balanced. It can be quite good, but not great. A good choice with melon, nectarines, peaches, or other fresh fruit. Look for Rocca Bernarda from Perusini Antonini, or Savorgnano from Picogna M. Zompitta.

Piesport(er), Gm. Piesport is one of the best wine towns of the Middle (Mittel) Mosel. These wines at their best are delicate, light, and distinguished, with a fragrant perfume. Piesporter vineyards: Domherr, Gärtchen, goldtröpfchen, Grafenberg, Güntherslay, Falkenberg, Hofberger, Kreuzwingert, Schubertslay, Treppchen. Michelsberg is the Grosslage (general site). Piesport's most famous vineyard is Goldtröpfchen, "Little drop of gold." Important producers: Bischöfliches Konvikt, Reichsgraf von Kesselstatt, and Vereinigte Hospitien.

Pineau de la Loire Another name for the Chenin Blanc (see) grape.

Pinot Bianco The Pinot Blanc (see) grape in Italy is called the Pinot Bianco; in the Alto Adige (see) it is also known as the Weissburgunder. This variety is widely planted in northern Italy, predominantly in the north-eastern regions of Trentino-Alto Adige, Veneto, and Friuli-Venezia-Giulia. Most of the Pinot Bianco wines are undistinguished though some good ones are produced, notably Franciacorta (see). Some highly regarded Italian Pinot Biancos: from Friuli-Venezia-Giulia—Villa Russiz, Conti Formentini, Gradmir Gradnik, Doro Princic, Baronesse Tacco, Rocca Bernarda (Perusini Antonini), and Ronchi di Manzano; from Alto Adige—Josef Hofstätter and Herrnhofer; from Trentino—Fratelli Endrizzi; from Veneto—Luciano Ciuto; from Lombardy—Baroni Monti della Corta (Franciacorta), Lazzarini (Bianco del Rocolo), and Nino Negri (Castel Chiuro). Very few of these wines are seen in the United States, and those that are tend to be too old, tired, and with little redeeming value. It is unfortunate that the better ones are rarely found here in young enough vintages. These wines are dry, medium-bodied, and often a little low in acid. Serve with mixed seafood dishes or poultry or pasta with piquant sauces.

Pinot Blanc   A lesser grape similar in character to the noble Chardonnay (see). Pinot Blanc is grown in Burgundy, in Alsace, and in Germany, where it is known as Weissburgunder, Weisser Burgunder, and Clevner, in Italy as Pinot Bianco (see), in California, and some of the Balkan countries. The Pinot Blancs of California are in the style of a lightweight Chardonnay, with less class and distinction. Some California producers treat the grape like a Chardonnay, and age the wine in small oak cooperage. In these cases it can produce a rather distinguished wine, but is rarely worth the price. At least one Italian producer—Simonini—produces a wine labeled Pinot Blanc (Favonio), from grapes grown in Apulia, in the "heel" of Italy. To date, the wine hasn't been particularly distinguished, but shows promise.

Pinot Chardonnay   See Chardonnay.

Pinot Grigio See Pinot Gris.

Pinot Gris This grape variety is also called Pinot Grigio (in Italy), Ruländer (Germany, Italy, and Austria), Tokay d'Alsace (France), and Szürkebarát (Hungary). This grape produces its best wines in Baden (as the Ruländer) and in New York State (Dr. Konstantin Frank's Pinot Gris). Some good Pinot Grigios are produced in Italy. They are best when very young. Good producers in Friuli-Venezia-Giulia: Angoris, Marco Felluga, Gradmir Gradnik, Conti Formentini, Giovanni Scolaris, Villa Russiz, Barone Codelli, Morelli de Rossi, Tilatti cav. Isidoro, Tavagnacco e Dorigio (Casa Rossa), and Molin di Ponti (from the Cooperativa); in Trentino: Casteller del Poggio; and in Bolzano: Schloss Kehlburg. The Italian versions are best within a year of the vintage; like the Pinot Bianco, those seen here are often past their prime. Angoris is a notable exception, having lately been exporting its Pinot Grigio very young. The Tokay d'Alsace seems to age well, retaining its fruitiness for up to ten years. Hugel is a fine producer. The dry (Italian and Alsatian) versions go well with shellfish; others, with poultry dishes or fresh-water fish.

Pitigliano, Bianco di, It. A white wine made from Trebbiano, Greco, Malvasia, and Verdello grapes grown in the southern part of Tuscany. Pitigliano is dry, with medium body and moderate acidity. In its youth it can be pleasant, but rarely more. It finishes, like many Italian whites, on a somewhat bitter note. This bitterness increases with age; the wine should be drunk young while it retains its youthful freshness.

Pomino Bianco, It. A dry, fruity, medium-bodied white wine from Trebbiano, Malvasia, and Pinot Bianco grapes, produced in Tuscany by Frescobaldi. Drink very young with pasta in seafood sauces or mixed fish-fry.

Portugal The white wines of Portugal are not well known here, and deserve to be better known. Portugal's most popular white wine is Vinho Verde (see). Some of the wines of Lafões are reminiscent of Vinho Verde though less good. White wines are produced in a number of regions. Colares produces very little white, and it is of no particular distinction. Some light, fruity whites are produced at Obidos; at Santarém, dry, fruity white wines. One of the world's best Muscat dessert wines comes from Portugal (see Moscatel de Setúbal). The fortified dessert wines of Carcavelos are worth discovering. White wines are also produced in Dão, Bussaco, and Bucellas (see under individual listings).

Pouilly Blanc Fumé See Pouilly-Fumé.

Pouilly-Fuissé, Fr. The best wine from the Mâcon (see), Pouilly-Fuissé has more character and authority than the other wines of the region. The wine is greenish-gold in color, medium-bodied, dry and crisp, with a distinctive aroma. This wine is produced from Chardonnay grapes in the towns of Chaintré, Fuissé, Pouilly, Solutré, and Vergisson. Because of the demand for this wine, today it is usually overpriced. The wines of Pouilly-Loché, Pouilly-Vinzelles, and Saint-Véran (see individual listings) are all lesser wines, but being considerably less expensive, are better value. Even the wines of Meursault, which are generally more distinguished, are usually less expensive than Pouilly-Fuissé. Drink with turkey or game hens, chicken or veal. G. Duboeuf is a good producer.

Pouilly-Fumé, Fr.   A dry, white wine produced in the lower Loire valley around the town of Pouilly-sur-Loire (see) from Sauvignon grapes. It is pale in color with a flinty or smoky aroma, medium-bodied, fruity, and quite dry. Pouilly-Fumé is best within two or three years of the vintage, and in good years will live for five to six years. Drink with shellfish, sole, cod, bass, or other salt-water fish. Baron de Ladoucette (Château du Nozet) is one of the most highly regarded producers of the region. (See also Sancerre; Quincy; and Reuilly.)

Pouilly-Loché, Fr.   A Mâcon wine less well known, and less good, than Pouilly-Fuissé, but better priced. It is often a very fine value. Best consumed within two or three years of the vintage. Drink with salt-water fish or shellfish.

Pouilly-sur-Loire, Fr.   A small village in the lower Loire (see) producing wine from Chasselas and Sauvignon Blanc grapes. Wines from the Sauvignon are entitled to be labeled Pouilly-Fumé (see), and they are far superior to those labeled Pouilly-sur-Loire. When young and fresh the Pouilly-sur-Loire wines can be pleasant drinking with fish and poultry dishes. These wines should always be inexpensive.

Pouilly-Vinzelles, Fr.   A wine from the southern Mâcon region adjoining Pouilly-Fuissé (see). Like Pouilly-Loché (see) it is less distinguished, but also considerably less expensive than Pouilly-Fuissé. For that reason it is a fine substitute. It is best within a few years of the vintage. Drink with fish dishes or shellfish.

Preignac, Fr.   One of the five communes of Sauternes (see). Its best-known vineyards: Château Suduiraut and Château de Malle.

Premières Côtes de Blaye   See Blaye.

Premières Côtes de Bordeaux, Fr.   One of the controlled appellations of origin (AC) of Bordeaux producing semi-sweet to sweet wines. Loupiac (see) and Sainte-Croix-du-Mont (see), within the Premières Côtes region, have their own appellations. Cadillac (see) is one of the best-known communes. The less sweet wines go well with poultry or veal in cream sauces, the sweet wines with fruit.

Preuses, Les, Fr.   A grand cru Chablis (see).

Prosecco di Conegliano   See Prosecco di Conegliano-Valdobbiadene.

Prosecco di Conegliano-Valdobbiadene, It.   These wines, sometimes labeled Prosecco di Conegliano or Prosecco di Valdobbiadene, are produced from Prosecco grapes grown in Treviso in the Veneto region of northeastern Italy. Those labeled Superiore di Cartizze are from a specially delimited zone. The Proseccos are made in various styles, from very dry to quite sweet, still and sparkling. They are generally low in alcohol and fruity with a slightly bitter finish. These wines can be enjoyable when very young, but are rarely sold in the United States young enough. The food match depends on the style; the driest goes well with salt-water fish or shellfish, the off-dry or Amabile (semi-sweet) with poultry or pasta in cream sauces, and the Dolce (sweet) with dessert. Nino Franco and Pino Zardetto are respected producers.

Provence, Fr.   An area in southern France producing a lot of common, ordinary wine. It also produces some respectable wines worth knowing, though, in these inflationary times. Look for Bandol, Bellet, and Cassis (see individual listings); these are wines to accompany spicy fish dishes or bouillabaisse. Palette (see) and Côtes du Lubéron (see), for fish or poultry in piquant sauces. The wines labeled Côtes de Provence usually are of lesser quality, but they are also less expensive. None of these wines ages well. Drink cold, while very young.

Puligny-Montrachet, Fr. Puligny, now Puligny-Montrachet for its most famous vineyard, is one of the most important white wine villages of Burgundy. The wines of Puligny are greenish-gold in color with a rich, fruity bouquet. They are wines of breed and distinction. The Puligny wines have strength and authority but less so than those of Le Montrachet. Overall, the wines labeled simply with the village name, Puligny-Montrachet, are less consistent and reliable than those of its southern neighbor, Chassagne-Montrachet. Besides the grand cru vineyards of Montrachet, Chevalier-Montrachet, Bâtard-Montrachet, and Bienvenue-Bâtard-Montrachet, Puligny's best vineyards are Caillerets and Combettes. Other premier crus: Chalumeaux, Champ-Canet, Charmes, Clavoillons, Clos du Meix, Folatières, Garenne, Hameau de Blagny (see Blagny), Perrières, Pucelles, Referts, Sous le Puits, and Truffière. Fine producers: Jacques Prieur, Domaine Leflaive, Louis Latour, Louis Jadot. These wines make a fine accompaniment to roast veal, turkey, or cornish game hens.

Puttonyos See Tokaji.

Q.b.A. See Qualitätswein.

Q.m.P. See Qualitätswein mit Prädikat.

Qualitätswein, Gm. Short for Qualitätswein bestimmter Anbaugebiete (Q.b.A.), meaning quality wine of a designated region. Q.b.A. wine can be, and most likely is, chaptalized—that is, sugar can be added to increase the alcoholic level if the grapes didn't achieve enough natural sugar. The label must give, at the least, the name of the region—one of the eleven designated regions, or Anbaugebiete (see), where 75% of the grapes were grown. More specific information such as the town or vineyard producing the wine may be specified. A Q.b.A. wine from a given producer should always be his most inexpensive "quality" wine.

Qualitätswein mit Prädikat, Gm. The highest classification of German wine. These Q.m.P. wines must be made from fully ripened grapes; no sugar can be added. A predicate also appears on the label: Kabinett, Spätlese, Auslese, Beerenauslese, Trockenbeerenauslese. Eiswein may appear in combination with any of these five terms (see individual listings). These wines, according to German law, are fine wines of special quality. At a minimum, the wine must be from a single subregion (Bereich) in one of the eleven regions (Anbaugebiete). If the bottle carries a vineyard name, at least 75% of the grapes must be from that vineyard.

Quarts de Chaume, Fr. One of the most famous vineyards of the Coteaux du Layon (see) district of Anjou (see), producing rich, golden dessert wines from overripe Chenin Blanc grapes. This 120-acre vineyard is made up of Château de Bellerive, Château de Surronde, and Ancien Domaine du Dr. Bernard. At one time this vineyard belonged to Dr. Bernard, who rented it out for one-quarter of the production, reserving the right to choose the quarter he preferred. Quarts de Chaume has a flowery bouquet, and although high in alcohol gives the impression of lightness. It is more delicate than the Sauternes, and also less sweet. It may be compared to a lighter Barsac. Like the Sauternes and Barsacs, Quarts de Chaume is made from grapes graced with the "noble mold" (see Botrytis cinerea). (See also Bonnezeaux.)

Quincy, Fr. A wine produced in the lower Loire near Sancerre and Pouilly-Fumé from the same grape variety, Sauvignon Blanc, that produces those wines. This dry, crisp wine is in fact like a lesser Sancerre. Quincy would go well with salt-water fish or shellfish. (See Sancerre; Reuilly; Pouilly-Fumé.)

Rabaud-Promis, Château, Fr. A first-growth Sauternes (see) from Bommes.

Rabaud-Sigalas, Château, Fr. A first-growth Sauternes (see) from Bommes.

Radgonska Ranina See Tigrovomleko.

Rajnai Grašvina, Yg. Rhine Riesling (see Riesling).

Rajnai Rizling, Hn. Rhine Riesling (see Riesling).

Rajnski Rizling, Yg. Rhine Riesling (see Riesling).

Randersacker(er), Gm. Randersacker is the second most important wine town of Franconia (Franken) after Würzburg. Randersackerer vineyards: Dabug, Marsberg, Pfülben, Sonnenstuhl, Teufelskeller. Important producers: Bayerische Landesanstalt, Bürgerspital zum Heiligen Geist, Ernst Gebhardt, Juliusspital, Bruno Schmitt, and Paul Schmitt.

Rasteau, Fr. One of the controlled appellations (ACs) of

France for a fortified dessert or aperitif wine. This AC is allowed for both a Vin de Liqueur (see) and a Vin Doux Naturel (see). The village of Rasteau is in the southern Côtes du Rhône. Rasteau is a good wine to drink with nuts. Good producers: Bressy, Charavin, Colombet, Nicolet, and Vache.

Rauenthal(er), Gm. Rauenthal is one of the finest wine towns of Germany, producing wines of the highest overall quality of the Rheingau. Rauenthalers are famous for their distinction and breed, their fruit and spice, balance and complexity, strength and delicacy. Baiken is the most famous estate. In great years these wines are among Germany's best. Other Rauenthaler vineyards: Gehrn, Langenstück, Nonnenberg, Rothenberg, and Wülfen. Grosslage (general site): Steinmächer. This Grosslage also takes in the towns of Eltville, Martinsthal, Niederwalluf, Oberwalluf, and other not so well known villages. Probably very little wine labeled Rauenthaler Steinmächer ever comes from Rauenthal. Important producers: Schloss Eltz, Schloss Schönborn, Schloss Reinhartshausen, Langwerth von Simmern, and Staatsweingut.

Ravat Blanc or **Ravat 6** This French-American hybrid grape produces full-bodied wines. They can be pleasant, rarely more than that.

Ravello Bianco, It. One of the better white wines from Campania produced from vineyards near the Amalfi Coast. This wine is a bit low in acidity and doesn't keep well. It is best drunk while young and fresh, with seafood salads or stews. Try it with Zuppa di Vongole. Caruso is a reliable producer.

Rayne-Vigneau, Château, Fr. A first-growth Sauternes from the villages of Bommes. It is one of the best vineyards of Sauternes (see).

Recioto Bianco, It. Similar to, if not the same as, Recioto di Soave (see). Masi produces a good Recioto Bianco.

Recioto di Soave, It. This wine, made from overripe grapes, ranges from semi-sweet to sweet. It is rich and concentrated, with a velvety texture, a pleasing taste, and a dry finish. Recioto di Soave goes well with fruit and nuts.

Regaleali, It. This Sicilian wine is one of the best white wines of southern Italy. Regaleali is produced by Conte Tasca d'Almerita from grapes grown on his estate in the province of Palermo. It is dry and full-bodied. Drink with seafood in piquant sauces.

Reichensteiner This new German hybrid is a cross between Müller-Thurgau X Madeleine d'Angevine X Calabreser-Fröhlich.

Renski Riesling, Yg. Rhine Riesling (see Riesling).

Renski Rizling, Yg. Rhine Riesling (see Riesling).

Reserve du Prieur, It. A white wine from Grenache grapes produced in the Val d'Aosta of northwestern Italy.

Réserve Exceptionelle See Grand Réserve.

Réserve Speciale See Grand Réserve.

Retsina, Gc. White wines flavored with resin. They smell like something to clean your paintbrushes in. These wines are definitely an acquired taste. Try them with spicy or oily dishes, or Greek salad.

Reuilly, Fr. A dry, crisp white wine made from Sauvignon Blanc grapes in the upper Loire region. As it is little known in this country, and similar to Sancerre and

Pouilly-Fumé, Reuilly can be a very fine value. Best within two to three years of the vintage. A good choice to accompany shellfish.

Rheingau, Gm. Near Mainz, the northward-flowing Rhein quite suddenly changes direction and veers south and west for about twenty miles until Bingen, where it turns northward once again. This region, the Rheingau, includes approximately 7,000 acres of vines, mostly Riesling (76%); Müller-Thurgau comprises 11%, and Sylvaner another 5%. The vineyards are planted on slopes with a southern exposure. They are sheltered from the cold north winds by the Taunus hills. The Rheingau produces wines of the highest average quality of any of the eleven designated wine regions (Anbaugebiete) of Germany. These wines are elegant, well-balanced, and firm, with the most distinctive character of all the Rhein wines. The best of the Rheingaus have a richness of flavor and a complexity of bouquet which sets them apart from the other wines of Germany. The Rheingau has one subregion (Bereich), Johannisberg, and ten general sites (Grosslagen): west to east—Steil, Burgweg, Erntebringer, Honigberg, Gottesthal, Deutelsberg, Mehrhölzchen, Heiligenstock, Steinmächer, and Daubhaus. The most important towns, most of which are world famous: Rüdesheim, Geisenheim, Johannisberg, Winkel, Hattenheim, Hallgarten, Erbach, Kiedrich, Eltville, Rauenthal, and Hochheim (see individual listings; see also Steinberger; Johannisberg, Schloss; and Vollrads, Schloss). Among the most important producers in the Rheingau: Domdechant Werner, Hessische Forschungsanstalt, Landgräflich Hessisches, Graf Matuschka Greiffenclau, Fürst von Metternich, G. H. von Mumm, Schloss Eltz, Schloss Groensteyn, Schloss Schönborn, Schloss Reinhartshausen, Langwerth von Simmern, Staatsweingüter, Geh. Rat Julius Wegeler Erben, and Weingut der Stadt Frankfurt.

Rheinhessen, Gm. One of Germany's most important wine-producing regions (Anbaugebieten) covering nearly 54,000 acres. Only the Palatinate (Rheinpfalz) produces more wine. The Rhein is on the eastern and northern boundaries, the Nahe on the west, and the Palatinate on the south. The Rheinhessen wines are soft, light, pleasant, and mild, with an engaging charm when young. The best are distinguished and elegant. Nearly all of the almost 160 towns of Hessia have vineyards. The Müller-Thurgau comprises 36% of the plantings; the Sylvaner, 28%. The best wines, as elsewhere, are made from the Riesling, which covers only 5% of the total. Even Scheurebe is planted more extensively—6%. German wine law recognizes three Bereich (subregions) for the Rheinhessen: Bingen, Nierstein, and Wonnegau. From a quality standpoint, Nierstein, in the northeast, is the most important. Bingen is in the northwest, and Wonnegau in the south. The best towns are Dienheim, Nackenheim, Nierstein, and Oppenheim (see individual listings). Important producers: Anton Balbach Erben, Richard Beyer, Dr. Dahlem Erben K. G., Gunderloch-Lange, Gunderloch-Usinger, Louis Guntrum, Freiherr Heyl zu Herrnsheim, Landes-Lehr-und Versuchanstalt, Franz Karl Schmitt, Gustav Adolf Schmitt, Geschwister Schuch, Heinrich

Seip, Reinhold Senfter, Carl Sittmann, Staatlichen Weinbaudomänen, J. u. H. A. Strub, and Villa Sachsen. (See also Worms and Liebfraumilch.)

Rheinpfalz   See Palatinate.

Rheinriesling   See Riesling.

Rhine Riesling   See Riesling.

Rhine Wine, U.S.   A generic wine term with about as much meaning as California or New York "Chablis" (virtually none). Usually a soft, slightly sweet, and bland wine with little character. Drink well-chilled with poultry or veal in cream sauces; also goes with pasta in cream sauces.

Rhône   See Côtes du Rhône.

Ribeauvillé, Fr.   One of the foremost wine towns of Alsace. Dambach is noted for its fine Riesling. Zahnacker is another good vineyard.

Ribolla   An Italian grape variety grown in Friuli-Venezia-Giulia (see).

Rieslaner   A hybrid grape variety from a Sylvaner and Riesling cross. One of the new German hybrids, formerly called Main Riesling.

Riesling   One of the noble grape varieties of the world. This variety is grown in most of the major wine-producing countries, and under a number of different names. In Germany and Alsace, the two areas where it does the best, it is known simply as Riesling. In many other countries, such as the United States, Australia, and Austria, it is known as Johannisberg Riesling, White Riesling, and Rhine Riesling. In the Balkan countries it is called Rajnski or Rajnai Rizling, Renski Rizling or Riesling. Other names: Weisser Riesling, Rössling,

Moselriesling, Niederlander, Klingelberger, Klein Riesling, Pfeffel, Riesling Renano, Ryzlink, and Renski.

In California, there is a very slim possibility that a wine labeled Riesling is in fact from the Riesling grape; most likely it is from the Sylvaner. Grey Riesling and Emerald Riesling are not Rieslings. Neither is Monterey Riesling. The true Riesling will be labeled either Johannisberg Riesling or White Riesling. Riesling is treated more like a generic wine term in California than a grape name, and it is deceptive. In Italy a wine labeled Riesling can be either the Rhein Riesling (Riesling Renano) or the Riesling Italico. Most likely it is the latter. This variety is not a true Riesling. In other countries the Riesling Italico is known as Olasz Rizling, Welsch Reisling, and Wälschriesling (see Welschriesling).

In Germany the Riesling produces light, delicate, fruity wines with a flowery or fruity perfume and a racy, lively acidity. These wines are made in styles ranging from off-dry to lusciously sweet. In Alsace the Riesling is king. The wines are fuller and drier than those of Germany. They also have more alcohol, and are crisp and fruity. While German Rieslings, from the Mosel and the Rhine, are best alone, as sipping wines, those from Alsace are food wines. They go well with poultry and fresh-water fish. The Rieslings of Austria are in between the German and Alsatian styles, being drier and fuller than the former but less so than the latter. Austrian Rhine Rieslings go well with pan-fried trout, perch, or other fresh-water fish. Young Italian Riesling Renanos from the Alto Adige can be quite enjoyable with chicken and fish. Generally these wines are crisp and relatively full-bodied. Australian Rhine Rieslings and California White or Johannisberg Rieslings are generally soft, mild, and fruity with a gentle touch of acidity. They go with chicken or fish dishes in cream sauces. New York Johannisberg Rieslings are similar to the Alsatians in style; the Rieslings from Washington State and Oregon are closer to the Austrian Rieslings.

Riesling Italico   See Welschriesling.

Riesling Renano   See Riesling.

Riesling X Sylvaner   See Müller-Thurgau.

Rieussec, Château, Fr.   A premier cru Sauternes (see) from the village of Fargues.

Rioja, Sp.   Rioja, in northern Spain, is primarily a red wine area, but some whites are also produced. Generally these wines spend too long in wood (casks), which causes them to dry out and lose their fruit. The best of these wines, such as the Viña Tondonia, can be interesting. These wines go well with mixed seafood stews or fish or shellfish in piquant sauces. Lately, the producers are beginning to bottle the whites soon after the vintage, giving the wines little or no wood aging. These wines are light to medium-bodied, off-dry, fruity, and fresh. They go well with chicken in cream sauces. Look for Señorial.

Ripley   Believe it or not, this native American variety is used to produce wine, pervasively grapey wine.

Riquewihr, Fr.   One of the best wine-producing towns of Alsace (see), noted for its fine Rieslings (see). Sporen and Kellenberg are noted vineyards.

Rivesaltes, Fr. A fortified dessert wine, VDN, produced in Roussillon. The best one is labeled Muscat de Rivesaltes. (See Vin Doux Naturel.)

Rizling See Riesling.

Rizvanac Bijeli See Müller-Thurgau.

Roche-aux-Moines, La, Fr. A fine vineyard in Savennières (see), producing some very fine dessert wines from Chenin Blanc grapes.

Rochefort-sur-Loire, Fr. A highly regarded wine-producing village of Anjou. Quarts de Chaume (see) is the most famous vineyard. These dessert wines—other than Quarts de Chaume—are labeled Coteaux du Layon (see).

Romer, Château, Fr. A second-growth Sauternes (see) produced in Fargues.

Rosette, Fr. An off-dry, sometimes semi-sweet wine produced in the Dordogne Valley near Bergerac. It is made from the same varieties used in Sauternes: Sémillon, Sauvignon, and a little Muscadelle.

Roussanne One of the white grape varieties used in the wines of Hermitage, Crozes-Hermitage, St.-Joseph, and St.-Péray.

Rousselet, Fr. These fruity wines can be quite agreeable when drunk young. They are named for the grape variety they are made from. Rousselet de Béarn is a well-known wine made from this variety. Drink it young.

Roussette An improved version of the Roussanne (see) grape variety.

Roussillon, Fr. A southern French district producing mostly ordinary wines. The best wines of this area are the fortified dessert wines (see Vin Doux Naturel): Banyuls (see), Côtes d'Agly (see), Côtes du Haut-Roussillon, Maury, and Rivesaltes (see).

Rüdesheim(er), Gm. One of the best and most famous wine villages—not only of the Rheingau (see), but of all Germany. Rüdesheimer wines are known for their full body, richness, and fruit. These wines are the softest of the Rheingaus. In lesser vintages, the wines of Rüdesheim are the most distinguished, the best of the Rheingau. In great (dry) years, they can be awkward. Rüdesheim, with its wine-garden-lined street, the Drosselgasse, is a major tourist site. The steepest vineyards here are planted on rocky terraces. The wines from this area are labeled Rüdesheimer Berg followed by a site name: Roseneck, Rottland, Schlossberg. Other Rüdesheimer vineyards: Bischofsberg, Drachenstein, Kirchenpfad, Klosterberg, Klosterlay, Magdalenenkreuz, and Rosengarten. Rüdesheim is in the Grosslage (general site) Burgweg. Important producers: Julius Espenschied, Hessische Forschungsanstalt, G. H. von Mumm, Fritz Rücker Erben, Schloss Eltz, Schloss Groensteyn, Schloss Reinhartshausen, Schloss Schönborn, Staatsweingüter, and Geh. Rat Julius Wegeler Erben.

Rueda, Sp. A white wine from northern Spain; it is one of Spain's better white wines, from the Verdejo Blanco grape.

Ruländer See Pinot Gris.

Rully, Fr. A dry, fruity white wine from the Côte Chalonnaise (see). It is most agreeable when young, especially with fish or poultry dishes. Some noted premier crus: Grésigny, Margotey, Raboursay, and Raclot.

Rumania This Balkan country produces some interesting dessert wines as well as some respectable table wines. The grape varieties grown here are Italian Riesling, Traminer, Ruländer, Furmint, Sauvignon, Neuburger, Muscat Ottonel, Fetească, and other local varieties. Cotnari (see) and Murfatlar (see) are two of Rumania's noted dessert wines, the former more famous than the latter. Bănat, Drăgăşani, Dealul-Mare, Tîrnave, and Focşani are noted wine-producing areas. Valea Câlugărească is particularly esteemed for its Muscat Ottonel; Tîrnave, for its table wines. Teremia and Tomnatec are the most highly regarded areas of Banat. Dealul Mare produces table wines; Tohani and Sāhăteni are the most highly esteemed wine regions. Most of the wine seen here is too old and tends to be dull and uninteresting as well as often oxidized.

Ruppertsberg(er), Gm. The best wines of Ruppertsberg are among the best of the Palatinate. About 20% of the 400-odd acres are planted to Riesling. Ruppertsberger vineyards: Gaisböhl, Hoheburg, Linsenbusch, Nussbien, Reiterpfad, Spiess. Hofstück is the Grosslage (general site) name; Mittelhaardt Deutsche Weinstrasse, the Bereich (subregion). Important producers: Bassermann-Jordan, Bürklin-Wolf, R. von Buhl, Dr. Deinhard, Dietz-Matti, Carl Josef Hoch, Jos. Reinhardt, Siben Erben, Eugen Spindler-Weingut Lindenhof, Wilhelm Spindler, and Weingut Hahnhof.

Rust(er), Au. A district in the Burgenland region of Austria.

Some good wine towns include Breitenbrunn, Don-
nerkirchen, Eisenstadt, Gross-Höflein, Jois, Klein-
Höflein, Mörbisch (famous for its Muscats), Neusiedl,
Oggau, Purbach, St. Georgen, St. Margarethen, and
Widen. Wines are produced here from the Wälschries-
ling, Neuburger, Pinot Blanc or Weisser Burgunder,
Traminer, and Grüner Veltliner varieties. Wines from
Rust labeled Ruster Ausbruch are made from overripe
Muscat Ottonel and Furmint grapes and are richly
sweet. These wines go well with fruit.

Ruwer, Gm.   A small area (about 500 acres) included in the
Mosel-Saar-Ruwer wine region. The wines of the
Ruwer are the lightest in body, the most delicate and
fragile of all the great wines of the world. They tend to
be drier than those from the Mosel proper, and have a
haunting, flowery, spicy perfume noted for its complexity. They do share a slight sparkle, or spritz, with the
other Mosel wines. Practically all of the Ruwer is
planted to Riesling. Nearly half of this acreage is in
Kasel (see). The most highly esteemed wine towns of
this area: Maximin Grünhaus, Eitelsbach (now labeled
Trier), Waldrach, and Kasel. The most highly regarded
producers: Von Schubert (Maximin Grünhaus), W.
Tyrell (Eitelsbacher Karthäuserhofberg), Bischöfliches
Konvikt, Bischöfliches Priesterseminar, and Kesselstatt.
(See Maximin Grünhaus, Eitelsbach, Trier, and Kasel.)

Rynsky   See Riesling.

Ryzlink   See Riesling.

Saar, Gm.   Part of the Mosel-Saar-Ruwer region (Anbaugebiete). In all but the best years, the Saar wines

are hard, thin, acidic, and lacking balance. But when the sun smiles on the Saar, these wines are elegant, noble, with an underlying steeliness and austerity that makeş them extraordinary drinking. In dry, sunny years, the Saar wines are rivaled only by the best wines of the Ruwer in the entire Mosel-Saar-Ruwer region. The best wine-producing towns of the Saar are Ayl, Oberemmel, Ockfen, Saarburg, Serrig, Wawern, and Wiltingen (see individual listings). The best villages have in total 1,500 acres of vines, nearly all Riesling. Other villages include Filzen, Kanzem (see), Mennig, and Pellingen. The most highly regarded vineyard of the Saar is Scharzhofberg (see), in Wiltingen. Noted producers in the Saar: Bischöfliches Konvikt, Bischöfliches Priesterseminar, Dr. Fischer, Friedrich Wilhelm Gymnasium, Hohe Domkirche, Von Hövel, Reichsgraf von Kesselstatt, Joseph Koch, Egon Müller, Edmund Reverchon, Adolf Rheinart Erben, Staatlichen Weinbaudomänen, Thiergarten Georg Fritz von Nell, Vereinigte Hospitien, and Van Volxem.

The Saar-Ruwer area includes the Grosslagen (general sites) Römerlay and Scharzberg. Scharzberg (see) is not to be confused with Scharzhofberg, the single best vineyard of the Saar. (See also Mosel and Ruwer.)

Saarburg(er), Gm. Saarburg is one of the most important wine villages of the Saar (see). Saarburger vineyards: Antoniusbrunnen, Bergschlösschen, Fuchs, Klosterberg, Kupp, Laurentiusberg, Rausch, Schlossberg, and Stirn. Saarburg is in the Grosslage (general site) Scharzberg. Rheinart is a good Saarburger producer.

Saint-Aubin, Fr. One of the lesser wine villages of the Côte de Beaune (see). If young enough, and cheap enough, these wines can be fair value. (See Burgundy.)

Saint-Emilion   See Ugni Blanc.

Saint-Joseph, Fr.   This northern Côtes du Rhône wine region is known mainly for its red wines, but a fair quantity of white wine is also made, from Marsanne and Roussanne grapes. It is medium-bodied, dry, and fruity. This wine goes well with fresh-water fish. It is best when drunk within a few years of the vintage. The white St.-Josephs of Chapoutier and Paul Jaboulet are often seen in the United States. There are a number of good small producers: Desbos, Florentin, Grippat, Marsanne, and Trollat, to name a few.

Saint-Macaire   See Côtes de Bordeaux.

Saint-Péray, Fr.   A village in the northern Côtes du Rhône known mostly for its sparkling wine. Some pleasant, medium-bodied, off-dry, white, still wines are made here from Marsanne and Roussanne grapes. A good choice for fresh-water fish. Clape, Mathon, Milliand, Teyssere, and Viogeat are noted producers. Verilhac is an important shipper.

Saint-Romain, Fr.   A secondary village in the Côte de Beaune (see).

Saint-Saphorin   See Vaud.

Saint Véran, Fr.   One of the ACs (controlled appellations of origin) in the southern Mâcon (see) producing a wine similar to those of Pouilly-Fuissé, Pouilly-Loché, and Pouilly-Vinzelles (see individual listings). Saint Véran should always be less expensive than Pouilly-Fuissé.

Sainte-Croix-du-Mont, Fr.   A full-bodied dessert wine, similar to, though not as good as, Sauternes. It is produced east of the Sauternes district from the same grape varieties—Sémillon, Sauvignon Blanc, and a small amount of Muscadelle. (See Cérons; Sauternes; Barsac; Monbazillac; Sainte-Foy-Bordeaux.)

Sainte-Foy-Bordeaux, Fr.   Sweetish white Bordeaux wines from the same grapes used in Sauternes—principally Sémillon and Sauvignon Blanc. (See Barsac; Cérons; Monbazillac; Sainte-Croix-du-Mont.)

Ste. Michelle, U.S.   A Washington State winery producing a good Gewurztraminer and one of America's best Johannisberg Rieslings.

Sampigny-les-Maranges, Fr.   A southern Côte de Beaune (see) village producing some agreeable white wines. Very little is sold under the village name.

San Marino   The world's smallest country (less than 25 square miles), completely surrounded by Italy, produces a white Moscato quite similar to the Italian Moscatos. The wine production here, like the country, is quite minuscule.

San Martin Vineyard, U.S.   A Santa Clara winery that produces a sweet Johannisberg Riesling with low alcohol (10%).

Sancerre, Fr.   Along with Pouilly-Fumé (see), Sancerre produces the best wines of the Upper Loire. This wine, made from the Sauvignon Blanc grape, is dry, crisp, and fruity. It would be a good choice to drink with shellfish or other fruits of the sea. Best within four or five years of the vintage. Clos la Perrière Archambault, Comte Lafond, and Brochard are good producers.

Santenay, Fr.   A village in the Côte de Beaune (see) below Chassagne-Montrachet. Some good white Burgundies are produced in Santenay from both Chardonnay and Pinot Blanc. In general, these wines are relatively inexpensive.

Saumur, Fr.   This wine town in Anjou produces white wines from the Chenin Blanc grape. Usually medium-bodied and fruity with a nice acid balance, these wines range from off-dry to semi-sweet. They are perhaps the driest of all the better Anjou wines. But even these wines usually have a hint of sweetness, and in better years can be lusciously sweet. Due to this slight sweetness, the Samur wines go well with poultry and veal in cream sauces.

Saumur, Coteaux du   See Saumur.

Sauterne, U.S.   American white wines named for the Sauternes district of France, and that is where the similarity ends. American Sauterne is made from a variety of grapes; the quality and style vary widely also. True Sauternes is always sweet. American Sauterne can be dry or sweet. If the word Château or Haut appears on the label (of an American Sauterne), the wine is probably sweet; if not, it could be either.

Sauternes, Fr.   One of the greatest wine districts of the world, producing rich, luscious dessert wines from overripe Sémillon and Sauvignon Blanc grapes (some Muscadelle is also planted) that have been concentrated and enriched by the *pourriture noble* (see Botrytis cinerea).

The grapes are picked in successive passes through the vineyard. At each picking, the workers pick only those bunches that are overripe and covered with the noble mold. The resultant wine is sweet and luscious, with a velvety texture and a honeyed, fruity bouquet. These wines are high in alcohol, sometimes exceeding 14%, and age well because of this high sugar and alcohol.

These wines cannot be made every year. They are more subject to the vagaries of the weather than the dry wines because the grapes are harvested so late and because they need warm, sunny days combined with enough dampness in the autumn for the noble mold to form on the bunches.

Five villages make up the Sauternes district: Barsac, Bommes, Fargues, Preignac, and Sauternes itself. The wines of Barsac (see) are the lightest and least sweet of the Sauternes. In 1855 the wines of Sauternes were classified by the Bordeaux wine brokers according to quality, prestige, and, most important, price. This classification recognizes one premier grand cru— Château d'Yquem (see Yquem, Château d'), eleven premier crus, or first growths, and twelve second growths.

The premier crus: Châteaux La Tour-Blanche, Lafaurie-Peyraguey, Haut-Peyraguey, and Rayne-Vigneau (all in Bommes), Suduiraut (Preignac), Coutet and Climens (in Barsac), Guiraud (Sauternes), Rieussec (Fargues), Rabaud-Promis and Sigalas-Rabaud (both in Bommes).

The second growths: Châteaux Myrat, Doisy-Daëne, Doisy-Dubroca and Doisy-Védrines (Barsac), d'Arche and Filhot (Sauternes), Broustet, Nairac, Caillou, and Suau (Barsac), de Malle (Preignac), Romer (Fargues), and Lamothe (Sauternes).

Because of the extra labor required during the harvest and the greatly reduced yield per acre, Sauternes can never be cheap. But, as sweet wines are out of fashion today, they are, relatively speaking, among the greatest bargains in wine.

Drink these wines chilled with fresh fruit such as strawberries, peaches, or nectarines, or alone as sipping wines.

Sauvignon   See Sauvignon Blanc.

Sauvignon Blanc   The grape variety of Sancerre, Pouilly-Fumé, Quincy, and Reuilly (see individual listings) in the upper Loire, and one of the two major white grape varieties of Bordeaux (see Bordeaux; Graves; Sauternes; Barsac). This variety also does very well in California, where some very fine examples have been produced by Spring Mountain, Caymus, Oakville (now out of business), Sterling, and Stonegate. Some California producers label their Sauvignon Blanc wines Blanc Fumé. Robert Mondavi and Dry Creek make good Blanc Fumés. Sauvignon Blanc produces wines with a grassy, herbaceous aroma that is quite distinctive. At their best these wines are medium-bodied, dry, and fruity, with a fine balance and a lingering finish. Next to Chardonnay, Sauvignon Blanc is California's best white-grape variety, producing wines of class and distinction. A good choice with shellfish or salt-water fish in piquant sauces.

Sauvignon is also grown in Italy. It is not one of Italy's best varieties. But in the hands of a good producer, some very good Sauvignon wines are made, mostly in Friuli-Venezia-Giulia: Angoris, Attems, Doro

Princic, Formentini, Gradnik, Molin di Ponte, Della Roncada, Schiopetto, and Villa Russiz. The Sauvignon di Monte San Pietro from Bologna can also be quite good. These wines don't age as well as the Sauvignons from France or California. Sauvignon wines recognized by Italian wine law (DOC) are produced in the Alto Adige, Terlano, Colli Berici, Collio Goriziano, Colli Orientali del Friuli, Isonzo, and Colli Bolognesi. Italian Sauvignon goes well with fish or pasta in piquant sauces.

The Sauvignon is also planted in Hungary, Rumania, and Yugoslavia.

Sauvignon Vert A rather undistinguished grape variety generally used for blending. A handful of California producers bottle a Sauvignon Vert wine.

Savennières, Fr. One of the major wine-producing villages of the Coteaux de la Loire in Anjou. The wines of Savennières, made from Chenin Blanc, are the fullest and driest of the Anjou whites. These wines have a fragrant, fruity aroma, and a fine fruity flavor. They would be a good choice to accompany roast veal or turkey. La Coulée de Serrant is the most highly regarded vineyard of Savennières, followed by La Roche-aux-Moines. Châteaux de Savennières, d'Epiré, and Clos du Papillon are other good estates. Mme. Joly produces a fine Coulée de Serrant.

Savigny-les-Beaune, Fr. This northern Côte de Beaune (see) village produces some good white Burgundies that are often fine value.

Savoie, Fr. The best wines of this region in eastern France are Crépy (see) and Seyssel (see). The other wines

produced here are labeled Vins de Savoie. When young
and fresh they can be pleasant enough.

Scharzberg, Gm. The Grosslage (general site) name allowed
for towns in the Saar (see) district. Not to be confused
with Scharzhofberg (see).

Scharzhofberg(er), Gm Scharzhofberg, in the Saar, is one of
the best vineyards of Germany. In dry years these
wines are extraordinary, with a fragrant, flowery
perfume, a delicacy and lightness unsurpassed by any
other wine. The major Scharzhofberger producers:
Hohe Domkirche—labeled as Dom Scharzhofberger;
Reichsgraf von Kesselstatt; Joseph Koch; Egon
Müller—the most highly regarded; Carl Rautenstrauch;
and Vereinigte Hospitien, von Hövel, and van Volxem.
Wines labeled Wiltinger Scharzberg are not from
Scharzhofberg. Scharzberg is the Grosslage (general
site) for the Saar.

Scheurebe A hybrid grape variety from a Sylvaner and
Riesling cross. The Scheurebe is planted mostly in the
Rheinhessen. It produces wines with a pronounced
bouquet, fruity flavor, and lively acidity.

Schloss, Gm. Castle, or château. Some very fine wine estates
are Schloss properties—Schloss Vollrads, Schloss Johannisberg, etc. (See individual listings under the estate
name, e.g., Vollrads, Schloss.)

Schlossböckelheim(er), Gm. Schlossböckelheim is one of the
two most important wine towns of the Nahe (see). It is
also one of the two Bereich (subregions); a wine labeled
Schloss Böckelheim can come from anywhere in the
southern Nahe. Schlossböckelheimer vineyards: Felsen-
berg, Heimberg, In den Felsen, Königsfels, Kup-

fergrube, and Mühlberg. Important producers: August Anheuser, Rudolf Anheuser, Carl Finkenauer, Reichsgraf von Plettenberg, and Staatlichen Weinbaudomänen.

Scuppernong The most noted variety of Muscadine or *Vitis rotundifolia* grapes, producing strong-flavored wines with a musky aroma and a flavor some find reminiscent of fresh plums. Scuppernong was used to produce the first American wines. It is grown in the southern states—Alabama, Florida, Georgia, Mississippi, North and South Carolina, and Tennessee.

Sec, Fr. Dry.

Secco, It. Dry.

Seeweine, Gm. The wines produced along the northern shore of Lake Constance, or the Bodensee, are referred to as Seeweine ("lake wines"). (See Baden.)

Seewinkel, Au. An area in Burgenland, Austria. The vineyards here are planted in sandy soil, and the wines are known as "sand wines" (Sandweine). The name of the grape variety the wine is made from follows the name Seewinkel on the label.

Sémillon One of the two major white wine grapes of Bordeaux. More Sémillon than Sauvignon Blanc is planted in the Sauternes district than in the Graves since it is more susceptible to *Botrytis cinerea* (see). The wines produced in California from this variety lack the class of those from the Sauvignon Blanc grape. The Sémillon wines also tend to be somewhat deficient in acid. They generally range in style from off-dry to sweet and have a distinctive aroma. Sémillon is also planted in Yugoslavia, Australia, South Africa, New

Zealand, and some of the South American countries. In New South Wales, Australia, it is known as Hunter Valley Riesling. Chilean "Riesling" is often made from the Sémillon. Sémillon is at its best when combined with Sauvignon Blanc in the wines of Sauternes (see).

Septimer   A new German hybrid from a cross of Gewürztraminer and Müller-Thurgau.

Serrant, Coulée de   See Savennières.

Serrig(er), Gm.   In very great vintages the wines of the Saar (see) Valley village of Serrig can be among the most outstanding of the entire Mosel-Saar-Ruwer district. But these years don't come often enough. Like most wines of the Saar, these wines are often thin, harsh, and acidic. Serriger vineyards: Antoniusberg, Heiligenborn, Herrenberg, Hoeppslei, König Johann Berg, Kupp, Schloss Saarfelser Schlossberg, Schloss Saarsteiner, Vogelsang, and Würtzberg. Serrig is in the Grosslage (general site) Scharzberg. Fine producers: Staatlichen Weinbaudomänen, Vereinigte Hospitien.

Sèvre-et-Maine   See Muscadet.

Seyssel, Fr.   One of the best wines of the Savoie district in eastern France. The Seyssel wines challenge Chablis and Muscadet for dryness. This bone-dry wine is a good accompaniment to shellfish. Clos de la Paclette is a good producer.

Seyval Blanc   A French-American hybrid grape that produces some agreeable white wines. They are best when young and fresh. Some claim this variety (Seyve Villard 5276) is the best white hybrid. It has an aroma and flavor reminiscent of apples. These wines are generally well-balanced with a crisp, green-apple-like acidity.

Seyval Blanc goes well with seafood of all kinds. Walter S. Taylor of Bully Hill Winery in New York State produces a particularly good example.

Seyve Villard 5276   See Seyval Blanc.

Sherry   See Montilla

Siegerrebe   A new German hybrid from a Madeleine d'Angevine and Gewürztraminer cross.

Sigalas-Rabaud, Château, Fr.   A first-growth Sauternes (see) from Bommes.

Silvaner   See Sylvaner.

Simi Winery, U.S.   An Alexander Valley (California) winery which produces a respectable Gewürztraminer.

Sipon   A Yugoslavian grape variety, thought to be the Furmint, grown mostly in Slovenia. Ljutomer Sipon is available in the United States, but it is usually too old and tired.

Soave, It.   Italy's most popular white wine. So popular, in fact, that more Soave is sold than is produced. Bottles of "Soave" with DOCs may be seen in retail stores selling for under $1.00. But considering the cost of bottles, corks, shipping, taxes, etc., one must question its authenticity. Wine laws notwithstanding, it still pays to look for the name of a reliable producer and shipper, in other words, a name you can trust. This means much more than a government "guarantee."

Soave is produced around the lovely walled city of Soave in Verona. This wine, like most Italian whites, is best when young, while it is still fresh and fruity. Soave is pale in color with an almond-like aroma. It is light to medium-bodied, dry and crisp, with a slightly bitter aftertaste. While most Soave is best within a year of the vintage, a few like Bertani are still good two or three years later. Masi is one of the best and most reliable producers. Soave is a wine to accompany salt-water fish or shellfish.

Solopaca, It.   A southern Italian white, from the Campania region. Solopaca is made from Trebbiano and Malvasia grapes, with the addition of other varieties. Despite its DOC, it is rather coarse, dull, and uninteresting. Drunk as young as possible, it could accompany spicy seafood dishes.

Somló, Hn.   One of the major wine districts of Hungary. Somló produces a highly regarded white dessert wine: Somlói Furmint. (See Hungary.)

Sonoma Vineyards, U.S.   A California winery which makes one of the best California Chardonnays in the lower price bracket.

South Africa   This country has taken advantage of modern technology to improve its white wines. Fermentation at low temperatures allows the wines to retain their freshness and fruit. Most South African wines are produced in the Cape province in the southwestern corner of the country. The major districts are Paarl and Stellenbosch. Dessert wines are produced in Little Karoo. Tulbagh, north of Paarl, produces some of the best whites of South Africa. Twee Jongegezellen is the most highly regarded estate here. Steen and Riesling are the major white grape varieties. Steen is believed to be related to the Chenin Blanc, or perhaps be the Chenin Blanc. Most wine growers in South Africa belong to the KWV (Ko-operative Wijnbouwers Ver-eniging). This cooperative controls over 90% of all the

South African wines exported. Some nonmember estates: Twee Jongegezellen (a good Steen and Riesling), Nederburg, Bellingham (both regarded for their Rieslings), Monis Wineries, Alphen, Bertrams, and Stellenvale.

Steen is made in two major styles—dry and off-dry. The off-dry is labeled "Late." South African white wines tend to be full-bodied and fruity. Though sometimes somewhat deficient in acid, they can be pleasant and enjoyable. These are food wines, good with poultry and veal dishes.

Spain   One of the major wine-producing countries of the world. The most important white wine regions are Rioja, Alella, Valencia, Ribeiro, Valdeorras, Panadés, La Mancha, Valdepeñas, Yecla, Galicia, Tarragona, Catalonia, Toledo, Albariño and Leon.

The best whites of Spain, according to the experts, come from Galicia, but these wines are not available here.

Spanish wines are generally labeled with a regional name, as well as a producer name. Not many of the classic grape varieties are planted in Spain.

The white wines of Spain are often dull and uninteresting; they usually spend too long in wood (casks), where they tend to become oxidized. But there are some good white wines produced in Spain, though few are seen here. There is reason to believe that technology will play an increasing role in Spanish viniculture, improving the quality of the Spanish whites. The white Señorial from Rioja is a good example of a Spanish wine that has been improved by technology. This wine is light, clean, and fresh. It doesn't have that heavy, stale, oxidized taste often associated with Spanish whites.

Spain produces some very fine aperitif, or after-dinner wines and Sherries. Montilla (see) and Manzanilla (see), while not table wines, can be drunk with certain types of food as well as sipped alone. (See Rioja.)

Spätlese, Gm. Literally, "late picking." Spätlese wines, like the other German quality wines with special attributes (see Qualitätswein mit Prädikat), must meet specific requirements. The grapes for the Spätlese must have achieved a minimum level of sugar. The Spätlese wines as a rule tend to be lightly sweet—sweeter than the Kabinetts, but drier than the Auslesen from the same vineyard.

Spätrot Another name for the Zierfandler, a Sylvaner-type grape grown in Austria; the grape used in the Gumpoldskirchner (see) wines.

Spring Mountain, U.S. A Napa Valley winery which produces some of California's best Chardonnay and Sauvignon Blanc wines.

Stag's Leap Wine Cellars, U.S. A Napa Valley winery which produces a good Johannisberg Riesling.

Steen A South African grape variety that some believe to be the Chenin Blanc.

Steinberg(er), Gm. The 62-acre Steinberg vineyard is considered by some the single best site in Germany. Steinberger at its best has few peers and no superiors. This wine is known for its power and authority, its fullness and depth of flavor, its distinction, breed, strength, and nobility. Not all the wines from the Steinberg vineyard share this distinction, only the better wines: the Spätlesen, Auslesen, Beerenauslesen, and Trocken-beerenauslesen. Those below the classification of Kabinett can be rather common.

The entire vineyard is owned by the German state; the labels bear the name Staatsweingüter. The vineyard is in Hattenheim on the Rheingau, but so famous and esteemed is this wine that the label simply reads Steinberger without the town name (see Hattenheim).

Steinwein   See Franconia.

Stellenbosch   See South Africa.

Sterling Vineyards, U.S.   A Napa Valley winery that makes a good Sauvignon Blanc. It also makes a white Cabernet Sauvignon.

Stonegate Winery, U.S.   A Napa Valley winery that produces a good Sauvignon Blanc.

Stony Hill Vineyard, U.S.   Some good Johannisberg Rieslings and a fine Chardonnay are produced at this Napa Valley winery.

Suau, Château, Fr.   A second-growth Sauternes (see).

Süd Tyrol   See Alto Adige.

Suduiraut, Château, Fr.   A first-growth Sauternes (see) from Preignac.

Superiore di Cartize   See Prosecco di Conegliano Valdobbiadene.

Sutter Home, U.S.   A Napa Valley winery that produces a very good white Zinfandel.

Switzerland   Vines are planted in many areas of this Alpine country but the most important are Valais, Vaud, and Neuchâtel (see individual listings). Chasselas is by far the most important white grape variety, known here as Fendant or Dorin. Other major grape varieties: Johannisberg (Sylvaner), Ermitage (Marsanne), Malvoisie (Pinot Gris), Johannisberg Riesling, Amigne, Arvine, and Humagne. Swiss wines tend to be light to medium-bodied, dry and crisp—food wines, rather than sipping wines. Often overpriced. (See also Bienne.)

Sylvaner   This grape variety produces wines similar to those from the Riesling (see) but with less flavor, less distinction, and less class. Sylvaner wines are light-bodied and mild in flavor, pleasant and agreeable. In Germany Sylvaner is generally known as Silvaner. It is also called Franken Riesling in Franconia, Oesterreicher ("Austrian") in the Rheingau, and Frankentraube ("Franconian grapes") in the Palatinate.

The Sylvaner does as well in Alsace as it does in Germany. Alsatian Sylvaner is a good wine to accompany hors d'oeuvres.

In California, Sylvaner is known as Riesling or Monterey Riesling, as well as by other names. In Switzerland Sylvaner is known as Johannisberg.

Sylvaner is also planted in the Balkan countries and northern Italy. In the Alto Adige of Italy, Abbazia di Novacella produces a good Sylvaner. Terlano and Valle Isarco also produce Silvaner wines.

Szilváni   The Hungarian name for the Sylvaner (see).

Szürkebarat   See Badacsony and Pinot Gris.

Tafelwein, Gm.   Table wine; the lowest category of wine under the new (1971) German wine laws. Rarely seen in the United States.

Talbot, Château   See Caillou Blanc.

Terlaner   See Terlano.

Terlano, It.   One of the major controlled denomination of origin (DOC) wines in the Alto Adige. A wine labeled simply Terlano will be from a blend of grapes. The following are allowed: Pinot Bianco, Riesling Italico, Riesling Renano, Sauvignon, and Sylvaner. Any wine labeled Terlano followed by a grape name must be made primarily from that variety. Any of the five listed varieties is allowed. These wines tend to be light to medium in body and sometimes a little low in acid. They are among the best white wines of Italy, and are best drunk within a year or two of the vintage.

Ticino, Sw.   A wine-producing region in the southern part of Switzerland (see).

Tiger's Milk   See Tigrovomleko.

Tigrovomleko, Yg.   A dessert wine, Radgonska Ranina, produced around the town of Kapela from overripe Ranina grapes. It is referred to as Tigrovomleko—"tiger's milk." Drink with fresh fruit or fruit salad.

Tocai   An Italian grape variety, believed to be related to the Pinot Gris (see), growing in Friuli-Venezia-Giulia, Veneto, and Alto Adige. It produces rather bland, common little wines which can be pleasant when young and fresh. Serve well-chilled with spicy poultry or seafood dishes.

Tocai di Lison, It.   A white wine from the Veneto region in northeastern Italy made from the Tocai grape. This wine tends to be neutral, lacking acid and charm. Drunk while young and fresh (within a year of the vintage), though, it can be pleasant. Classico Tocai di

Lison is from vineyards in the classic zone of this delimited area, but is no better than the non-Classico. Drink with poultry, seafood, or pasta with piquant sauces.

Tocai di San Martino della Battaglia, It. A Tocai wine from Lombardy. This wine tends to be fuller-bodied than the Tocai di Lison. It is rather common and flat. Serve well-chilled with spicy poultry and fish dishes, or with Costolette alla Milanese (a local veal dish similar to Wienerschnitzel).

Tokarie See Tokaji.

Tokaji, Hn. One of the world's greatest dessert wines produced in the Tokaj-Hegyalja district of northeastern Hungary in the Carpathian Mountains. It is made from Furmint and Hárslevelü grapes. The best Tokaji is richly sweet, with an intense bouquet and flavor, and is low in alcohol. Tokaji Eszencia is made from grapes affected by the "noble mold" (see Botrytis cinerea). These grapes are placed into baskets where the very weight of them crushes the berries beneath. The resultant juice, collected drop by drop, is the pure essence of the grape, Eszencia. Extremely little of this (very expensive) nectar is bottled as it is; much of it is used for adding into Tokaji Aszu. The essence, measured in *puttonys* (buckets of grapes), is added to the fermenting Tokaji Aszu, which is made from normally ripened grapes. The more puttonys, the richer the Tokaji. Five puttonyos is the richest. Tokaji Edes is a sweet wine, perhaps comparable to a Spätlese or an Auslese in sweetness. Tokaji Szamorodni, the least expensive and most common of the Tokaji wines, ranges from dry to semi-sweet. All of the Tokaji wines are bottled in small bottles, slightly larger than pint size. While the sweeter wines are low in alcohol, the drier ones (Szamorodni) can be quite high, reaching 13% or more. The Eszencia and Aszu of four to five puttonyos are wines to be served after dinner in small amounts, like a liqueur. The drier wines go with spicy fish dishes or poultry in sauces. As they tend to be somewhat madeirized, they can be served as an aperitif (like a Sherry or Montilla).

Tokay   See Pinot Gris.

Tokay d'Alsace   See Pinot Gris.

Torgiano Bianco, It.   This wine, sometimes labeled Torre di Giano, is made in Umbria from the Trebbiano and other varieties. Usually coarse, bland, and neutral, if drunk very young can be a pleasant accompaniment to poultry or veal in piquant sauces. Serve very cold. Lungarotti is a good producer.

Torricella, It.   A white Tuscan wine made by Barone Ricasoli. Drunk while young and fresh, it can be pleasant. Serve with poultry or seafood, or pasta in light sauces.

Tour-Blanche, Château la, Fr.   At one time this first-growth Sauternes from the village of Bommes was more highly regarded. Today it doesn't justify its rank, and is overpriced as well.

Touraine, Fr.   One of the major wine-producing districts of the Loire. Vouvray (see) is its most famous growth. Chenin Blanc (see) is the major white grape variety. Montlouis (see) is another pleasant Touraine wine, as are Bourgueil (see), Chinon (see) and Jasnières (see).

Like Anjou (see), the best whites of Touraine are the sweet, luscious wines made from grapes affected by the "noble rot," Botrytis cinerea (see). The district of Touraine, named for the town of Tours, is chateau country. Both Amboise and Azay-le-Rideau, two famous Loire chateaux, are also known for their wines.

Touraine Amboise, Fr. This wine, from the Chenin Blanc, tends to be low in alcohol, and off-dry. It can be pleasant and charming. Touraine Amboise is similar in style to Montlouis (see). Drink with cold veal or poultry, or fresh-water fish.

Touraine Azay-le-Rideau, Fr. A white wine from the Touraine district of the Loire. It tends to be low in alcohol. A pleasant accompaniment to simple veal and poultry dishes, and fresh-water fish.

Touraine-Mesland, Fr. A white wine from the Touraine district of the Loire. It is made predominantly from the Chenin Blanc grape, but some Sauvignon is also used. It is low in alcohol, light-bodied, fruity, and rather fast-maturing (drink young).

Trakya See Turkey.

Traminac See Traminer.

Traminer This grape variety, reputedly the same as the Gewürztraminer (see), tends to be less spicy (*Gewürz* means spice). It is grown in Germany—Baden and the Palatinate (Rheinpfalz); Alsace, Austria, Yugoslavia— where it is known as Traminac; California—where sometimes what is called Traminer is actually the Red Veltliner; Italy—where it is called either Traminer or Traminer Aromatico (Gewürztraminer). This grape is believed to have derived its name from the Italian village of Tramin, now Termano in Süd-Tyrol (Alto Adige). The Traminer wines are generally lightly spicy, low in acid and alcohol.

Traminer Aromatico See Gewürztraminer.

Trebbianino Val Trebbia, It. This wine from Emilia-Romagna is made with some Trebbiano grapes, but not predominantly. It is generally light to medium-bodied, off-dry, and low in acid. When very young it can be pleasant and agreeable. Drink with fresh-water fish, flounder (sole) meunière, or poultry dishes.

Trebbiano, It. Also known as Ugni Blanc (see France; California) and St.-Emilion (see France). One of the most common grape varieties of Italy in both quantity and quality. This grape is used in many of the better-known Italian whites: Orvieto, Frascati, Est! Est!! Est!!!. Some regions—Emilia-Romagna, Latium, and Abruzzo, for example—have their own delimited zones for Trebbiano wines under Italian wine law (DOC). (See Trebbiano d'Abruzzo, Trebbiano di Aprilia.)

Trebbiano d'Abruzzo, It. An Italian white wine produced in the region of Abruzzo from Trebbiano grapes. This wine tends to be low in acid, coarse, bland, and common.

Trebbiano de Romagna, It. An Italian white produced in Emilia-Romagna from the Trebbiano grape. It tends to be heavy and awkward, lacking charm and balance. Generally bland and neutral, it can be pleasant when young and fresh. It is generally overpriced. Bacchini, Pasolini, Pezzi, and Marabini are noted producers.

Trebbiano di Aprilia, It. An Italian white produced from Trebbiano grapes in the region of Lazio. This wine is low in acid, fruit, and charm and has a bitterness at the end.

Trentino, It. In the southernmost part of Trentino-Alto Adige, the province of Trento produces some of Italy's most distinguished white wines. These wines are quite similar to those produced in Bolzano (see Alto Adige). The controlled denomination of origin (DOC) Trentino will appear on the label, generally followed by the name of the grape variety: Pinot (a blend of Pinot Bianco and Pinot Grigio); Riesling (Riesling Italico, Riesling Renano, Müller-Thurgau, and/or Riesling X Sylvaner); Traminer Aromatico; or Moscato. Vino Santo, a sweet wine with an underlying dryness, is also made here, labeled Trentino Vino Santo. These wines can also be labeled del Trentino. In this case the qualifier appears first—for example, Moscato del Trentino. (See also Valdadige.)

Trier(er), Gm. Prior to the new German wine laws (1971) one could say that although the wines of Trier were usually thin and acidic, in great years they could be light, fruity, and tart. Today, though, all the wines labeled Trierer no longer fit into this category. Now the name Trier has been stretched to include Avelsbach (see) and Eitelsbach (see). And in great years, the Eitelsbacher wines can be nothing short of extraordinary. Another generality that is true for most wines labeled Trierer, but not for the Eitelsbachers, is that they tend to mature quickly and fade fast. The wines of Eitelsbach will live. Important producers: Thiergarten Georg Fritz von Nell and Vereinigte Hospitien. The Staatlichen Weinbaudomänen and

Hohe Domkirche own vineyards in Avelsbach. Bischöfliches Konvikt has vineyards in Avelsbach and Eitelsbach. W. Tyrell owns the Karthäuserhofberg estate in Eitelsbach. There are now thirty vineyards under the label Trierer. Those labeled Trierer Karthäuserhofberg are from Eitelsbach. These wines are from the Ruwer Valley.

Trittenheim(er), Gm. Trittenheim is the southernmost wine town of note in the Mittel (Middle) Mosel. Although not generally as good as those from the central part—Wehlen, Bernkastel, Zeltingen, etc.—these wines are good value, being also less expensive than those. The Trittenheimer wines tend to be light and charming. They develop quickly and fade soon afterward. Important producers: Bischöfliches Priesterseminar, Freidrich Wilhelm Gymnasium, and Josef Milz, Jr. Trittenheimer vineyards: Altärchen, Apotheke, Felsenkopf, and Leiterchen.

Trockenbeerenauslese The richest, most luscious, and most expensive German (or Austrian) wine, especially when produced from Riesling grapes. The berries (*beeren*) are overripe and shriveled up, dried (*trocken*) on the vine. The grapes more often than not have been affected by the "noble rot," or Edelfäule (see Botrytis cinerea). Each grape yields only a few drops of concentrated nectar. This wine represents a tremendous amount of labor. And Trockenbeerenauslese can be made only in the very best years. These wines are finer and more delicate than the Sauternes (see), including the great Château d'Yquem (see). They are also rarer and more expensive. These special wines are best sipped by themselves, but may accompany ripe nectarines or peaches.

Turkey   Not much white wine of consequence is produced in Turkey. Trakya, a dry white from the Sémillon, is perhaps Turkey's best white wine.

Uerzig(er)   See Urzig(er)

Ugni Blanc   This grape is also called Trebbiano, in Italy, and St.-Emilion, in France. It produces rather common wines that seem somewhat ponderous, low in acid and in charm (see Trebbiano). It is also grown in California, where it is used for blending.

United States   Wine is produced in over thirty states. The most important, quality-wise, are California (see), New York (see), and Washington (see). A wider range of wines are produced in the United States than in any other country. Wines are also made from more species than in any other country. Basically American wines can be grouped in this way: wines from the European varieties (*Vitis vinifera*), native American varieties (including *Vitis labrusca, rupestris,* and many other species), and the French-American hybrids (developed in the last century from crosses between American varieties immune to phylloxera and European varieties). By far, America's best wines come from the European grapes. The native varieties have a pervasive grapey flavor and aroma described as being wild as a fox, hence "foxy." The major difference between wine from Concord, Catawba, etc., and grape juice is the alcohol. French-American hybrids, such as the Seyval Blanc, can produce some pleasant wines, but the best wines come from *Vitis vinifera* grapes, such as Johannisberg Riesling and Chardonnay. And the great majority of American wine is from the European varieties. Quality-wise, the United States is one of the most important wine-producing countries of the world.

Uruguay　Not much white wine from Uruguay is imported into the United States. These wines are rather common. By and large they are labeled for the region and/ or grape variety they are from. Sémillon and Pinot Blanc are important varieties. French-American hybrids and native American grapes are also grown.

Urzig(er), Gm.　Urzig, a small village in the northern part of the Middle (Mittel) Mosel, produces wines which are among the slowest-maturing of the Mosel wines. They can be acidicly tart in poor years, but when the sun smiles, they are among the best. In great years they are known for their liveliness and spice, particularly those from Würzgarten ("spice garden"). Other vineyards: Goldwingert. Urziger wines may use the subregion (Bereich) name Bernkastel. Schwarzlay is the Grosslage (general site) name. Fine producers: Geschw. Berres, Richard Josef Berres, Bischöfliches Priesterseminar, and Christoffel Erben.

Vacqueyras, Fr.　One of the Côtes du Rhône (see) Villages. The wines from Vacqueyras which meet the AC (Appellation d'Origine Contrôlée) requirements are sold as Côtes du Rhône Vacqueyras.

Valais, Sw.　One of the major wine regions of Switzerland in the upper Rhône Valley, east of Lake Geneva. Valais produces light, dry, fruity wines mostly from the

Fendant (see) grape. They are nice pleasant little wines, best within a few years of the vintage. Other grape varieties planted here: Johannisberg (the Sylvaner), Rhin (the true Riesling), Ermitage (Marsanne; see Hermitage), Malvoisie (Pinot Gris), Amigne, Arvine, and Humagne. The Malvoisie wines tends to be on the sweet side. The Amigne, Arvine, and Humagne wines are off-dry to lightly sweet. These wines are fuller in body than those from the Fendant, Johannisberg, or Rhin grapes. Drink the off-dry wines with poultry or veal in sauces, especially cream sauces, the dry wines with fresh-water fish or shellfish. All are best when young. Sion, Conthey, Ardon, and Vétroz are some of the villages of the Valais. Gilliard and Chevalier are reliable producers.

Valdadige Bianco, It. This wine, also known as Etschtaler, is produced from Pinot Bianco, Pinot Grigio, Riesling Italico, Müller-Thurgau, and other varieties grown in the provinces of Trento and Bolzano in Trentino-Alto Adige, and Verona in Veneto. The wine is off-dry, light to medium in body, soft and low in acid. When young and fresh it can be pleasant, but never more than that.

Val d'Aosta, It. This northwestern corner of Italy produces some of the best whites of Italy, none of which, though, are recognized by Italian wine law. Wines to look for: Blanc de Cossan, Blanc de La Salle, Blanc de Morgex, Le Vin du Conseil Petite Arvine, Reserve du Prieur, Passito di Chambave, and Malvoisie de Nus (see individual listings). In fact, not a single white wine from this region is recognized by Italian wine law (DOC)!

Valdepeñas See Spain.

Valdobbiadene See Prosecco di Conegliano-Valdobbiadene.

Valle Isarco, It. Also known as Eisacktaler, this is a controlled denomination of origin (DOC) in the northeastern part of Bolzano. This DOC applies to five white wines: Müller-Thurgau, Pinot Grigio (Ruländer), Silvaner, Traminer Aromatico (Gewürztraminer), and Veltliner. These wines are generally light and dry, low in alcohol, and with a nice acid balance. The Valle Isarco wines are best within two years of the vintage. (See Valdadige, Trentino, Terlano, and Alto Adige.)

Valmur, Fr. A grand cru Chablis (see).

Vaud, Sw. One of the major wine-producing cantons of Switzerland. The vineyards are planted on steep hillsides north of Lake Geneva. The predominant grape variety is the Fendant (see Chasselas), here known as the Dorin. This canton is divided into three viticultural districts: Lavaux, La Côte (see), and Chablais (see). The wines of La Côte are the lightest, those of Lavaux, a little fuller. The wines of Chablais are generally the driest. The most noted wines of Vaud come from Dézaley in Lavaux. Clos des Abbayes is one of the best estates in Dézaley. Clos du Renard is also a good estate. St.-Saphorin is another noted wine town here, as are Lutry, Chardonne, Epesses, Vevey, and Villette.

Vaudésir, Fr. This wine is considered by some the best of the seven grand crus of Chablis (see).

Veedercrest Vineyards, U.S. This Napa Valley winery has been experimenting with Johannisberg Riesling and Gewurztraminer wines in a variety of styles, sometimes blending grape varieties. It has produced a number of

late-harvest wines from overripe grapes. Some have
been successful; some not.

Velletri, It. One of the Castelli Romani (see) wines, generally
regarded as just behind Frascati (see) in quality. This
wine, like all the Castelli Romani wines, is best when
very young. Those available in the United States are
too old to be of interest.

Veltellini See Veltliner.

Veltliner An Austrian grape variety, also known as Grüner
or Frühroter Veltliner. It is the most widely cultivated
variety in Austria. It produces some pleasant, fruity
wines that are best when young. Most of the Austrian
plantings are in lower Austria. This variety is also
grown in the Balkan countries and in Italy. In California wines labeled Traminer are often from the
Veltliner grape. Generally these wines have a light
vinous aroma, low acidity, and are fast-maturing. They
are quite agreeable, especially with fresh-water fish in
light sauces. Some Veltliner is grown in northern Italy
also (see Valle Isarco).

Verdelet This grape, also known as Seibel 9110, is a French-
American hybrid variety. It produces some aromatic,
soft, and fruity wines that generally hold up well for
three to four years. Bully Hill's Verdelet Blanc is one of
the better ones. A wine to drink with chicken or veal in
cream sauces.

Verdicchio, It. One of Italy's most popular white wines,
often sold in an attractive amphora-shaped bottle.
Verdicchio is made predominantly from grapes of the
same name grown in the Marche region on the Adriatic

coast. *Verdicchio Castelli di Jesi* is generally regarded as the best, but any of the other Verdicchios can be as good or even better. Most seen here, though, is old and tired, with little to recommend it. Fazi Battaglia offers the best Verdicchio Castelli di Jesi seen in the United States. *Verdicchio di Matelica,* like the Castelli di Jesi, is made with some Trebbiano and Malvasia grapes. Dott. Attilio Fabrini produces a good *Verdicchio Pian delle Mura.* Verdicchio wines tend to be medium-bodied, quite dry, and when young pleasantly fruity with a refreshing acid balance. A good choice to accompany salt-water fish or shellfish. All Verdicchio should be consumed when young and fresh; this wine has a tendency to oxidize with age. Most Verdicchio tends to be overpriced.

Verduzzo This grape variety is indigenous to Italy. It is planted in Friuli-Venezia-Giulia, where it produces a medium- to full-bodied wine ranging in style from off-dry to semi-sweet. The best wines—the semi-sweet ones labeled Verduzzo Ramandolo—come from Colli Orientali. Look for the Verduzzo Ramandolo of G. B. Comelli. This variety is also planted in Veneto in the province of Treviso (see Piave). Look for the Verduzzo of Bianchi Kunkler. Verduzzo wines tend to be a little low in acid and so are best when young and fresh. In Grave del Friuli they are fuller and drier than in the other areas. Look for Domenico Casasolo and Perusini Antonini, two respected producers. The off-dry style goes well with poultry or fish in cream sauces, or pasta with cream sauce; the sweeter styles, with fruit.

Vergennes This native American grape variety is generally used to produce off-dry white wines, with, naturally, the grapey foxiness of the native varieties.

Vergine Valdichiana, Bianco, It. A Tuscan wine from Trebbiano and Malvasia grapes. It is a medium-bodied wine ranging from off-dry to semi-sweet, and finishes on a bitter note. Drink, very young, with pasta dishes with cream sauces (all' Alfredo, alla Panna, etc.).

Vermentino di Alghero, It. A white Sardinian wine with a flowery, fruity aroma, and a clean, fresh, fruity taste. It is light to medium in body and has a light sparkle. This wine is best when young, while it is fresh and charming. Sella e Mosca Vini produces a Vermentino di Alghero, which is one of Italy's best whites.

Vermentino di Berchidda, It. A white wine from Vermentino grapes produced in Sardinia.

Vermentino di Gallura, It. A Sardinian white wine from Vermentino grapes. It is generally medium-bodied, dry, soft, low in acid, and has a slightly bitter aftertaste.

Vermentino di Oristano, It. A white Sardinian wine, reminiscent of a Montilla (see). It makes a nice aperitif. It is high in alcohol and low in acid. A fortified (Liquoroso) style is also made. Drink with hors d'oeuvres or soups.

Vermentino di Savona, It. A white wine from Vermentino grapes produced in Liguria in northwestern Italy.

Vernaccia This Italian grape variety is planted in Sardinia and Tuscany.

Vernaccia di San Gimignano, It. This Tuscan wine is regarded by some writers as one of Italy's best dry white wines. In this country, though, the Vernaccia di

San Gimignano tends to be bland, neutral in character, and with a slightly cooked aroma and flavor caused by bad pasteurization. Unlike many Italian whites, this wine at its best reputedly improves with age. Since tastes vary, some might prefer it with a few years in bottle, but it loses fruit, and the bitterness at the end becomes more apparent. It is made from Vernaccia grapes, believed to be a Greek variety. The wine tends to be off-balance, lacking in acidity. Served well-chilled within a year of the vintage, though, it can be agreeable with spicy fish dishes. Pietrafitta is perhaps the most highly regarded producer of Vernaccia di San Gimignano.

Vespaiolo   A white grape variety grown in the Breganze (see) area of Veneto.

Victoria, As.   One of the major wine-producing areas of Australia (see). Great Western is one of the major wine districts of Victoria. Most of the vineyards in Great Western are owned by Seppelt. These wines are labeled with a place name followed by a generic name (Burgundy, Chablis, etc.) or grape variety name. Place names include Arawatta, Chalambar, Moyston, and Rhymney. Château Tahbilk at Tahbilk produces some agreeable white wines, including a white Marsanne (the grape of Hermitage, St.-Joseph, and other areas of the northern Côtes du Rhône).

Vigne Blanche   See Clos Blanc de Vougeot.

Vin Blanc, Fr.   White wine.

Vin de Liqueur (VDL), Fr.   A fortified dessert wine. Brandy is added before fermentation; consequently the grape juice and brandy are fermented together.

Vin de Paille   See Paille, Vin de.

Vin du Conseil Petite Arvine, Le   See Conseil Petite Arvine, Le Vin du.

Vin Doux Naturel (VDN), Fr.   VDNs are fortified wines; brandy is added to stop the fermentation thereby preserving some of the sugar in the wine and increasing the alcoholic content. (See Beaumes de Venise; Rasteau.)

Vin Jaune, Fr.   A deep golden dessert wine with a somewhat nutty flavor produced from overripe grapes in the Jura (see) district in eastern France. Drink as an aperitif, or after dinner with nuts.

Vin Santo, It.   A dessert wine produced in many parts of Italy, the most notable being those from Tuscany, Bolzano, and Veneto. These wines are made from overripe grapes which after picking are often left to dry on straw mats or wicker frames to concentrate the juice still further. Vin Santo is fermented in rather an unusual fashion. The grapes are pressed, and the juice run into small barrels. These barrels are kept in an attic room beneath the roof. Here the wine ferments through the summer. When the weather cools, the fermenting slows down and the wine "sleeps" during the cold winter. In the spring it begins to ferment again. This cycle continues for about five years, after which the wine is filtered and bottled.

This wine was at one time called Vin Pretto, and there are differing stories telling how it came to be called Vin Santo. According to one story, it was at a banquet in 1349 held to bring together the eastern and western divisions of the Catholic church that the wine got its name. At the end of the repast, Vin Pretto was poured. Cardinal Bessarione, primate of the Greek Orthodox church, tasted the wine and thought he recognized a wine from his own country. "This is Xantos," he declared. The Florentines in attendance thought he had sanctified their wine, calling it "Santo," and were so pleased with the compliment they have been calling it Vin Santo ever since.

There is a slightly different version of this story which again credits Cardinal Bessarione for naming, or renaming, the wine. On tasting the golden liquid, he is said to have remarked, "Ma questo e un vino santo" (But this is a holy wine).

The third story offers a somewhat more prosaic explanation for the unusual name. It seems that the pressing of grapes for Vin Santo takes place at Easter season, during Holy Week.

Vin Santo is amber-colored, velvety in texture, and sweet, but with a pleasing dry finish. It is high in alcohol, but is unfortified. Drink as an aperitif or after dinner with nuts or fruit.

Vin Santo di Gambellara, It. A Vin Santo (see) produced in Veneto from Gambellara grapes.

Vinho Verde, Pr. A light-bodied wine, low in alcohol (9-10%), and with refreshing acidity. The "green wine" is produced in the province of Minho in the northwestern part of Portugal. Sometimes described as "crackling," this wine often has a light sparkle. Vinho Verde is best when very young, and goes well with salt-water fish or shellfish.

Vini del Piave See Piave.

Vinifera Wine Cellars   See Frank, Dr. Konstantin

Vino Bianco, It.   White wine.

Vino Blanco, Sp.   White wine.

Vino Santo   See Vin Santo.

Viognier   The white grape variety used to produce the wines of Château Grillet (see) and Condrieu (see).

Viré, Fr.   One of the villages of the Côte Maconnaise, entitled to label its wine Mâcon Viré or Mâcon Villages Viré. Prosper Maufoux produces a good one.

Visperterminen, Sw.   An unusual wine produced in the Valais region of Switzerland near Sierre from grapes grown at a 4,000-foot altitude. Best drunk when young, the Visperterminen wines go well with simply prepared fresh-water fish.

Vollrads, Schloss, Gm.   This 91-acre estate is the largest privately owned vineyard of the Rheingau, owned by Graf Matuschka-Greiffenclau. In great vintages this wine is not often surpassed. It is rich and fruity with great breed. The vineyard is about 90% Riesling; some Müller-Thurgau is also planted. Schloss Vollrads uses color-coded capsules on its bottles to designate the quality of the wines: Q.b.A—green and green with gold; Kabinett—blue and blue with gold; Spätlese—pink and pink with gold; Auslese—white and white with gold; Beerenauslese—gold; and Trocken-beerenauslese—gold with a neck label.

Volnay, Fr.   One of the less well known wine-producing towns of the Côte de Beaune in Burgundy, producing mostly red wines. Some whites are also produced, and represent fine value. Most is sold as Meursault.

Vouvray, Fr.   The best-known wine district of Touraine, producing wines ranging from off-dry to richly sweet. In poor years the Chenin Blanc grape produces thin, acidic little wines. In great years, when the sun shines and Botrytis cinerea (see) strikes, the wines are rich, thick, and luscious. The sweet wines tend to live for decades. The off-dry style is a good choice to drink with fish or poultry, especially in cream sauces. The sweeter style is best with fresh fruit or drunk by itself. Clos du Bourg, Domaine des Bidaudières, La Père Drard, and Ackerman Laurance are some good names to look for.

Wachau, Au. This wine-producing district of lower Austria in the Kamp Valley is noted for its Rhine Rieslings, with pronounced bouquet and flavor. The predominant variety here, however, is the Grüner Veltliner, producing some fine wines. Other varieties include Müller-Thurgau, Muskat Ottonel, and Neuburger. The best wines come from Dürnstein Krems, Loiben, Spitz, and Weissenkirchen.

Wachenheim(er), Gm. Wachenheim is one of the four best wine towns in the Palatinate (see). These wines, while less fine than those from Forst and Deidesheim, are in that same noble class, particularly those from the Riesling grape. The Riesling wines are noted for their body and finesse. The best of them, in the very finest years, are much sought after. Most of the Wachenheimer vineyards, though, are planted to Sylvaner. The Riesling covers about 25% of the town's 840 acres. Reichsrat v. Buhl, Dr. Bürklin-Wolf, Dr. Dienhard, K. Fitz-Ritter, and Wilhelm Spindler are highly respected producers. Vineyards: Altenburg, Belz, Bischofsgarten, Böhlig, Fuchsmantel, Gerümpel, Goldbächel, Königswingert, Luginsland, Mandelgarten, Odinstal, Rechbächel, and Schlossberg. Wachenheim is within three Grosslagen (general sites): Mariengarten, Schenkenböhl, Schnepfenflug.

Wälschriesling   See Welschriesling.

Washington, U.S.   This state has only begun to come into its own as a premium wine producer. Some very fine white wines, particularly the Johannisberg Rieslings, have come out of the Yakima Valley. These wines are more in the style of Austrian or Alsatian Rieslings than Californian, with refreshing fruit acidity which gives them the balance expected of a fine Riesling. Because they are fuller in body than the German Rieslings, due to their higher alcohol, these wines are more food wines than sipping wines. Drink the Rieslings with poultry, especially chicken, hot or cold, or fresh-water fish, such as trout or pike. Other white varieties are planted here also and, by and large, are higher in acidity than those from California. Ste. Michelle Vineyards is a good producer.

Wehlen(er), Gm.   Wehlen, perhaps the best wine town in the Middle (Mittel) Mosel, produces Rieslings known for their delicacy and richness, their flowery bouquet and exquisite balance. They have been described as perfection itself. And, indeed, at their best, there are none better, and few as fine. The most famous vineyard of Wehlen, and one of the most highly regarded of Germany, is Sonnenuhr (sundial). The most highly regarded producer of Sonnenuhr and of Wehlen is J. J.

Prüm. His Auslesen (see) are among the most-sought-after wines of Germany and, naturally, among the highest in price. Other Wehlener vineyards: Abtei, Hofberg, Klosterberg, Klosterhofgut, and Nonnenberg. The Grosslage (general site) is Münzlay. Other noted producers: the Bergweilers—Adams, Licht, and Pauly; Dietz, Hauth-Kerpen, Peter Prüm, Sebastian Alois Prüm Erben, Zach. Bergweiler-Prüm Erben, Schneider, St. Nikolaus Hospital, Dr. H. Thanisch, Dr. Weins Erben, Weyer-Hauth, Stephan Studert Mentges.

Weinviertel, Au. The largest wine-producing district of Lower Austria (Niederösterreich), producing some good Grüner Veltliners and Müller-Thurgaus, notably those from Ravelsbach. Weisser Burgunder and Traminer are also grown. Pulkau, Retz, and Röschitz are known for their Grüner Veltliner wines.

Weissburgunder See Weisser Burgunder.

Weisser Burgunder The German and Austrian names for the Pinot Blanc grape (see). In Germany this grape is planted in Baden, the Palatinate, and Rheinhessen. The wines by and large are light golden in color, low in acid, and relatively high in alcohol. A good wine for spicy seafood or chicken in piquant sauces. It is also planted in northern Italy where it is also known as Pinot Bianco (see).

Welschriesling This grape variety is known as Wälschriesling in Austria, Germany, and some Balkan and Central European countries. Other names for this grape are Riesling Italico or Italian Riesling, and Italijanski Rizling, Grašvina, Grašica, Laški Riesling, Olaszrizling (these names are used in Hungary, Yugoslavia, and

other Central European countries). Welschriesling
wines lack the balance and elegant delicacy as well as
the intensity of fruit and bouquet of the true Rieslings
(see). With very few, if any, exceptions the wines are
dull, but when young and fresh they are a good
beverage with fish dishes. As these wines are rather dry,
they would go with salt-water as well as fresh-water
fish. They also go well with cold white meats.

Wente Brothers, U.S. A California winery that produces a
Chardonnay at good value in the lower price range.

White Pinot Some California wineries label their Chenin
Blanc (see) as White Pinot.

White Riesling Another name for the German Riesling (see
Riesling) in California.

Wiltingen(er), Gm. Wiltingen is without question one of the
finest wine towns on the Saar (see), producing elegant,
balanced Rieslings. In fine years the Wiltinger wines
are known for their bouquet, finesse, and steeliness.
The best vineyard of Wiltingen, and of the entire Saar,
is Scharzhofberger. There are those who say that in
great years it is the best vineyard in Germany. Other
vineyards: Braune Kupp, Braunfels, Gottesfuss, Hölle,
Klosterberg, Kupp, Rosenberg, Sandberg, Schlangen-
graben, Schlossberg. The general site (Grosslage) is
Scharzberg. But be wary; the names Scharzberg and
Scharzhofberg sound and look similar, but the similarity ends there. Scharzberg can be used on any wine
from Wiltingen; Scharzhofberg, only on wines from
that great vineyard. Respected producers: Apollinar
Joseph Koch, Bischöfliches Priesterseminar, Graf zu

Hoensbroech, Hohe Domkirche, von Hövel, Reichsgraf von Kesselstatt, Egon Müller, George Fritz v. Nell, Vereinigte Hospitien, and von Volxem.

Winkel(er), Gm. One of the most famous vineyards of the Rheingau (see) is in Winkel: Schloss Vollrads. The entire property is owned by Graf Matuschka-Greif-fenclau. This excellent wine is known for its elegance and distinction. Other Winkeler vineyards: Bienengarten, Dachsberg, Gutenberg, Hasensprung, Jesuitenberg, Klaus, and Schlossberg. Other producers of note: Blümlein, A. v. Brentano, Geromont, Jakob Hamm, Landgräflich-Hessisches, Krayer, G. H. v. Mumm, and Schloss Schönborn.

Wintrich(er), Gm. Wintrich produces some reliable Mosel wines. Though lacking the breed of those from Wehlen and Bernkastel, the Wintricher wines offer very fine value. Being little known, they don't fetch the higher prices of those well-known towns. Freiherr v. Schorlemer is a major producer who is quite reliable. Wintricher vineyards: Geierslay, Grosser Herrgott, Ohligsberg, Sonnseite, Stefanslay. Wintrich is in the Grosslage (general site) Kurfürstlay.

Winzenheim(er) Gm. The wines of Winzenheim, a fine wine-producing town on the Nahe (see), are no longer sold under the Winzenheimer name. They have been assigned, under the new (1971) German wine laws, to Kreuznach (see), its more famous neighbor. This hasn't done anything to improve their quality, but perhaps has to improve their reputation, or so it is apparently hoped. Vineyards to look for: Berg, Honigberg, Rosenheck, Schild, from such producers as Herf und Engelsmann Erben, Reichsgräflich v. Plettenberg, or Dr. Joseph Höfer Schlossmühle.

Winzergenossenschaft, Gm. A cooperative cellar owned by the wine producers.

Winzerverein, Gm. A wine producers' cooperative.

Worms(er), Gm. The most famous vineyard in Worms, at the southern edge of the Rheinhessen (see), is the Liebfrauenstift (see) Kirchenstück, believed to have lent its name to Liebfraumilch (see). Today parts of this vineyard are owned by Freiherr Heyl zu Herrnsheim, Langenbach, and Valckenberg.

Württemberg, Gm. One of the eleven wine regions (Anbaugebiete) of Germany. Württemberg produces red and white wine in almost equal amounts. This region produces table wines, unlike the Mosel and the Rheingau, which produce delicate wines best enjoyed without food. In this region there are 140 cooperatives, responsible for approximately 80% of the entire harvest of Württemberg, a very high percentage for a German region. Württemberg is south of Franconia (see) and produces similar wines. These wines are fuller, drier, and have less breed than those from the Rhein and Mosel regions. Major white varieties here include Riesling, Sylvaner, and Müller-Thurgau. Traminer and Ruländer do especially well here. Many of the newer hybrids are also planted. In this Anbaugebiete there are three subregions (Bereich): Remstal-Stuttgart, the southernmost area; Württembergisch Unterland; and Kocher-Jagst-Tauber, the northernmost. Producers worth looking for: Gräflich v. Bentzel-Sturmfeder,

Fürst zu Hohenlohe-Ohringen, Gräflich von Neipperg, Brüssele Schloss Kellerei Graf Adelmann, Staatliche Lehr-und Versuchsanstalt, and Württembergische Hof-kammer-Kellerei. The Württemberg wines are rarely seen outside Württemberg, but they are worth looking for. They represent good value.

Würzburg(er), Gm.   Würzburg is the most famous wine town of Franconia (see) with the most famous vineyard of the region, Stein. This 400-acre vineyard is the largest in Germany. The Würzburger wines are dry and austere with a fullness of body uncommon in Germany. These are food wines—pork, veal, sausages, poultry, fish—they all go well with these wines in the flat flagons *(bocksbeutel)*. Noted producers: Bayerische Landes-anstalt, Bürgerspital zum Heiligen Geist, Juliusspital (these three producers own approximately half of the Würzburger Stein vineyard). Other Würzburger vine-yards: Abtsleite, Innere Leiste, Kirchberg, Pfaffenberg, Schlossberg, and Stein/Harfe.

Würzer   One of the new hybrids, a cross between Gewürz-traminer and Müller-Thurgau producing Traminer-like wines that are often used for blending.

Xarello, Sp.   A grape variety producing white wines; grown in Catalonia near Barcelona.

"Y," Château, Fr.   A dry wine produced from Sauvignon and Sémillon grapes at Château d'Yquem (see Yquem, Château d'). It is an off-dry, lightly golden, full-bodied wine. Château "Y" has been made since 1959, but only in certain vintages, partly in answer to the growing popularity of dry whites and the declining popularity of sweet wines. This wine has the AC (Appellation d'Origine Contrôlée) Bordeaux Supérieur.

Yakima Valley, U.S. The premier grape-growing region of Washington State. This area produces some good white wines (see Washington).

Yalumba, As. A noted vineyard in the Eden Valley of South Australia (see), 35 miles northeast of Adelaide.

Yquem, Château d', Fr. The ne plus ultra Sauternes (see). Château d'Yquem was classified in 1855 as a premier grand cru classé, the single highest classification of any of the classified châteaux. The wine is produced from the grapes of successive pickings. On each pass through the vineyards, only the ripest and most heavily botrytised grapes are picked (see Botrytis cinerea).

This is, of course, an expensive process. Adding to the expense is the very low yield per acre. While the red wine and dry white wine estates of Bordeaux average 350 to 400 gallons per acre, Château d'Yquem produces less than one-third that amount. Because of the overripe condition of the grapes, each berry yields very little juice.

Château d'Yquem is a rich golden color, with a bouquet of honey and fruit. It is luscious and creamy in texture, very fruity, and lingers long on the palate. This wine is a fine accompaniment to stoned fruits such as peaches and nectarines, and marvelous with strawberries.

At Château d'Yquem it was the custom, as at many estates, that the proprietor or lord of the manor give the order for the harvest to begin. It seems that in the middle of the last century, the Marquis de Lur-Saluces, owner of Château d'Yquem, was away when the grapes began to ripen. And before he returned, they had become overripe and begun to rot. Since no one else was authorized to give the order to pick, the grapes were left on the vines as all anxiously awaited the Marquis's return. In the damp autumn mornings a mold spread over the grapes, which had begun to shrivel up like raisins—moldy raisins. The Marquis belatedly returned, and dauntlessly ordered the grapes to be harvested, grapes the likes of which had never been picked there before. To the surprise of all, when the wine was made it was a rich, lusciously sweet nectar—a triumph. So prized was it that the Czar's brother bought up four barrels of that 1847 vintage for which he paid 10,000 gold francs, a tidy sum, then and now.

Yugoslavia This Eastern European country, for the most part, produces dull, uninteresting little wines. The whites, when served very cold, make a reasonable accompaniment to spicy seafood or poultry dishes. Yugoslavian wines, like those from the other Balkan countries, are generally labeled for their area of production and the grape variety they are made from. Slovenia, as well as producing almost half of the wine of Yugoslavia, is reputedly responsible for that country's best wines. Slovenia borders Friuli-Venezia-Giulia in northeastern Italy, and grows many of the same grape varieties: Malvasia, here called Malvazija Istarska; Müller-Thurgau, or Rizvanac Bijeli; Pinot Bianco, or Beli Pinot; Pinot Grigio, called Burgundac Sivi or

Ruländer; Rhine Riesling, also known as Renski Riesling, Rajnski Rizling, and Rajnai Grašvina; Ribolla, here called Rebula; Sauvignon; Sylvaner, or Silvanec Zelini; Tocai, or Tokay (thought to be related to Pinot Gris); Traminer, or Traminac; and Wälschriesling, also called Laški Riesling, Italijanski Rizling, Grašvina, and Grašica.

Other white varieties grown in Yugoslavia: Chardonnay, or Burgundac Beli; Ezerjo; Furmint, also called Sipon, Moslavac Bijeli, and Pošipon; Grüner Veltliner, or Zleni Veltinac; Muskat Ottonel; Muskateller; Neuburger; Plavac; Radgonska Ranina (see Tigrovomleko); and Sémillon.

Maribor, Gornja Radgona, Ljutomer-Ormož (see Lutomer), and Ptny are the important white wine areas of Slovenia. Jeruzalem is a famous vineyard in the Ljutomer area. Brda and Goriška are also well-regarded wine-producing areas of Slovenia, producing dry, full-bodied wines from the Rebula grape.

The other wine-producing areas of Yugoslavia: Slavonia, Istria and Dalmatia, Herzegovina, Vojvodina, Serbia, Kosmet, and Macedonia.

In Slavonia, white wines are produced around the towns of Slavonski Brod, Kutjevo, Erdut, Ilok, Vukover, and Belji. These wines are fuller in body, higher in alcohol, and lower in acidity than those from Slovenia; and, of course, not as good.

In Dalmatia white wines are produced in Pošip, Maraština, Grk, and Vagava.

Mostarska Zilavka, considered by some authorities to

be Yugoslavia's greatest white wine, is produced in Herzegovina.

The white Yugoslavian wines seen in the United States tend to be too old. They are dull and uninteresting, often with an oxidized aroma and taste.

Yverdon, Sw. A noted wine-producing town at the western end of Lake Neuchâtel (see).

Yvorne, Sw. One of the better wine towns of Chablais (see), southeast of Lake Geneva.

Zagarolo, It. This wine, from Malvasia (see) and Trebbiano (see) grapes, ranges from dry to semi-sweet; more often than not, it has a touch of sugar. Zagarolo, named for the town 20 miles southeast of Rome where it is made, is similar to the Castelli Romani (see) wines and, like them, grows tired quickly. It is best consumed from cask in Zagarolo or in Rome.

Zell(er), Gm. Zell is the Bereich (subregion) for the Lower (Unter) Mosel. This town produces by and large some pretty mediocre wines, much of it sold under the name of the general site (Grosslage), Schwarze Katz. Zeller Schwarze Katz is a popular wine, but better buys from the Mosel can be found than the "Black Cat."

Zeltingen(er), Gm. Zeltingen is the largest wine-producing town on the Middle (Mittel) Mosel, and its average quality might just be the highest of all. It is not as widely acclaimed as Bernkastel, Piesport, and Wehlen, but some very fine values can be found, especially in an estate-bottled wine from a good producer. The Zeltinger vineyards: Deutschherrenberg, Himmelreich,

Schlossberg, and Sonne uhr. Some respected pro-
ducers: Ehses-Berres, Ehses-Geller, Friedrich Wilhelm
Gymnasium, Merrem, J. J. Prüm, and Freiherr v.
Schorlemer. The Zeltingers, along with the Braune-
bergers, are the fullest-bodied of all the Mosel wines.
They are known for their fullness and bouquet, though
are sometimes lacking in charm. Zeltingen is in the
Grosslage (general site) Münzlay; Bernkastel is the
Bereich (subregion).

Zierfandler, Au.   Also called Spätrot, this grape is thought to
be related to the Sylvaner (see).

Zilavka, Yg.   One of the best-known wines from Yugoslavia
(see).

Zwicker, Fr.   In Alsace (see) a blend of grapes containing any
of the common varieties is called Zwicker. These wines
are often sold in carafe. Most shippers' blends are
Zwicker wines. Although common, they can be pleasant when young and fresh.

Cross Reference

Australia
Barossa Valley
Chablis
Eden Valley
Glen Elgin
Hunter River Valley
Hunter Valley Riesling
Kaiserstuhl
Riesling
Sémillon
Victoria
Yalumba

Austria
Baden
Gewürztraminer
Grinzing(er)
Gumpoldskirchen(er)
Klevner
Krems(er)
Müller-Thurgau
Oggau
Pinot Gris
Riesling
Rust(er)

Seewinkel
Spätrot
Traminer
Trockenbeerenauslese
Veltliner
Wachau
Weinviertel
Weissburgunder
Weisser Burgunder
Welschriesling
Zierfandler

Bulgaria
Dimiat or Dimyat

Canada
Chablis
Concord

Cyprus
Agros

Czechoslovakia
Melnik

England
Müller-Thurgau

France
Abymes
Aligoté
Aloxe-Corton
Alsace
Ammerschwihr
Anjou
Annecy
Arbois
Arche, Château d'
Arlot, Clos de l'
Auxerrois
Auxey-Duresses
Azay-le-Rideau
Bandol
Banyuls
Baret, Château
Barsac
Bâtard-Montrachet
Bellet
Bergerac
Bergheim
Bienvenue-Bâtard-
    Montrachet
Blagny
Blanc
Blanc de Blancs
Blanc Fumé
Blanchots
Blanquette, Vin de
Blaye
Bommes
Bonnézeaux
Bordeaux
Botrytis Cinerea

Bougros
Bourg
Bourgogne
Bourgueil
Bouscaut, Château
Broustet, Château
Burgundy
Cadillac
Caillou, Château
Caillou Blanc
Cairanne
California
Carbonnieux, Château
Cassis
Cérons
Chablis
Chalon-sur-Saône
Chambolle-Musigny
Chardonnay
Charlemagne
Chassagne-Montrachet
Chasselas
Château
Château-Chalon
Château Grillet
Châteauneuf-du-Pape
Châtillon-en-Diois
Cheilly-les-Maranges
Chenin Blanc
Chevalier, Domaine de
Chevalier-Montrachet
Chinon
Clairette
Clairette de Bellegarde
Clairette du Languedoc
Clape, la
Clessé
Climens, Château

Clos
Clos, les
Clos Blanc de Vougeot
Clos des Mouches
Condrieu
Corbières
Corsica
Corton
Corton-Charlemagne
Costières-du-Gard
Côte Chalonnaise
Côte de Beaune
Côte de Nuits
Coteaux Champenois
Coteaux d'Aix
Coteaux d'Aix, Coteaux des
   Baux
Coteaux de l'Aubance
Coteaux de la Loire
Coteaux du Layon
Coteaux du Loir
Coteaux du Tricastin
Côtes d'Agly
Côtes-de-Bordeaux
Côtes de Buzet
Côtes de Duras
Côtes du Jura
Côtes du Luberon
Côtes du Rhone
Coutet, Château
Crépy
Criots-Bâtard-Montrachet
Crozes-Hermitage
Dame-Blanche, Château la
Demi-Sec
Doisy-Daëne, Château
Doisy-Dubroca, Château
Doisy-Védrines, Château

Doux
Edelzwicker
Elbling
Entre-Deux-Mers
Etoile, l'
Fargues
Fieuzal, Château
Filhot, Château
Fixin
Frontignan
Gaillac
Gewürztraminer
Givry
Grande Reserve
Graves
Graves de Vayres
Gros Plant
Guiraud, Château
Haut Benauge
Haut-Brion, Château
Haut-Peyraguey, Clos
Haut-Sauternes
Hermitage
Jasnières
Jura
Jurançon
Kaefferkopf
Kayserberg
Klevner
Knipperlé
Lafaurie-Peyraguey,
   Château
Lamothe, Château
Languedoc
Laville-Haut-Brion, Château
Limoux
Lirac
Loire

Loudenne, Château
Loupiac
Louvière, Château la
Mâcon
Malartic-Lagravière,
    Château
Malle, Château de
Malvasia
Melon de Bourgogne
Mercurey
Meursault
Mis en Bouteilles au Château
Mis en Bouteilles au
    Domaine
Moelleux
Monbazillac
Montagny
Montée de Tonnerre
Monthélie
Montlouis
Montrachet
Montravel
Monts-de-Milieu
Morey-St.-Denis
Müller-Thurgau
Muscadet
Muscat
Muscat d'Alsace
Muscat de Frontignan
Musigny
Muskat Ottonel
Myrat, Château de
Nairac, Château
Nuits-Saint-Georges
Olivier, Château
Paille, Vin de
Palette
Parnay, Château de

Patrimonio
Pavillon Blanc de Château
    Margaux
Pernand-Vergelesses
Pinot Blanc
Pinot Gris
Pouilly-Fuissé
Pouilly-Fumé
Pouilly-Loché
Pouilly-sur-Loire
Pouilly-Vinzelles
Preignac
Premières Côtes de
    Bordeaux
Preuses, les
Provence
Puligny-Montrachet
Quarts de Chaume
Quincy
Rabaud-Promis, Château
Rabaud-Sigalas, Château
Rasteau
Rayne-Vigneau, Château
Reuilly
Ribeauvillé
Riesling
Rieussec, Château
Riquewihr
Rivesaltes
Roche-aux-Moines, la
Rochefort-sur-Loire
Romer, Château
Rosette
Roussanne
Rousselet
Roussette
Roussillon
Rully

Saint-Aubin
Saint-Joseph
Saint-Péray
Saint-Romain
Saint-Véran
Sainte-Croix-du-Mont
Sainte-Foy-Bordeaux
Sampigny-les-Maranges
Sancerre
Santenay
Saumur
Sauternes
Sauvignon Blanc
Savennières
Savigny-les-Beaune
Savoie
Sec
Sémillon
Seyssel
Sigalas-Rabaud, Château
Suau, Château
Suduiraut, Château
Sylvaner
Tour-Blanche, Château la
Touraine
Touraine Amboise
Touraine Azay-le-Rideau
Touraine-Mesland
Traminer
Ugni Blanc
Vacqueyras
Valmur
Vaudésir
Vin Blanc
Vin de Liqueur
Vin Doux Naturel
Vin Jaune
Viognier

Viré
Volnay
Vouvray
"Y", Château
Yquem, Château d'
Zwicker

Germany
Ahr
Albalonga
Auslese
Auslesen
Auxerrois
Avelsbach(er)
Ayl(er)
Bacchus
Baden
Beerenauslese
Bereich
Bernkastel(er)
Bingen(er)
Bocksbeutel
Bodenheim
Botrytis Cinerea
Brauneberg(er)
California
Chasselas
Deidesheim(er)
Dhron(er)
Dienheim(er)
Dürkheim(er)
Ehrenfelser
Einzellage
Eiswein
Eitelsbach(er)
Elbling
Eltville(r)
Entkirch(er)

Erbach(er)
Erden(er)
Erzeuger-Abfüllung
Escherndorf(er)
Faber
Forst(er)
Franconia
Geisenheim(er)
Gewürztraminer
Graach(er)
Gutedel
Hallgarten(er)
Hattenheimer(er)
Hessische Bergstrasse
Hochheim(er)
Hock
Huxelrebe
Ihringen(er)
Iphofen(er)
Johannisberg(er)
Johannisberg(er), Schloss
Josephshof(er)
Kabinett
Kaiserstuhl-Tuniberg
Kallstadt(er)
Kanzem(er)
Kanzler
Kasel(er)
Kerner
Kiedrich(er)
Klevner
Knipperlé
Königsbach(er)
Kreuznach(er)
Kröv(er)
Lage
Liebfrauenstift
Liebfraumilch
Maximin Grünhaus(er)

May Wine
Mittelrhein
Morio Muskat
Mosel-Saar-Ruwer
Moselblümchen
Müller-Thurgau
Muskat Ottonel
Muskateller
Nackenheim(er)
Nahe
Neumagen(er)
Niederhausen(er)
Nierstein(er)
Norheim(er)
Oberemmel(er)
Ockfen(er)
Oesterreicher
Oestrich(er)
Oppenheim(er)
Ortsteil
Palatinate
Perle
Piesport(er)
Pinot Blanc
Pinot Gris
Qualitätswein
Qualitätswein mit Prädikat
Randersacker(er)
Rauenthal(er)
Reichensteiner
Rheingau
Rheinhessen
Rieslaner
Riesling
Rüdesheim(er)
Ruppertsberg(er)
Ruwer
Saar
Saarburg(er)

Scharzberg
Scharzhofberg(er)
Scheurebe
Schloss
Schlossböckelheim(er)
Seeweine
Septimer
Serrig(er)
Siegerrebe
Spätlese
Steinberg(er)
Sylvaner
Tafelwein
Traminer
Trier(er)
Trittenheim(er)
Trockenbeerenauslese
Urzig(er)
Vollrads, Schloss
Wachenheim(er)
Wehlen(er)
Weissburgunder
Weisser Burgunder
Welschriesling
Wiltingen(er)
Winkel(er)
Wintrich(er)
Winzenheim(er)
Winzergenossenschaft
Winzerverein
Worms(er)
Württemberg
Würzburg(er)
Zell(er)
Zeltingen(er)

Greece
Dekeleia
Demestica

Hymettus
Kokineli
Malvasia
Patras
Retsina

Hungary
Badacsony
Balaton
Botrytis Cinerea
Debröi Hárslevelü
Fehérburgundi
Furmint
Mór
Muskateller
Pinot Gris
Rajnairizling
Sauvignon
Somló
Szilváni
Tokaji
Welschriesling

Italy
Abboccato
Albana di Romagna
Albano
Alcamo or Bianco Alcamo
Alto Adige
Amabile
Aquileia
Bianchello del Metauro
Bianco
Biancolella
Blanc de Cossan
Blanc de Morgex
Blanc de la Salle
Breganze
Busa Calcara

Capena, Bianco
Capri
Castel del Monte
Castelli Romani
Cerveteri
Cinqueterre
Ciró Bianco
Colli Albani
Colli Berici
Colli Bolognesi dei Castelli
 Medioevali
Colli del Trasimeno
Colli Euganei
Colli Lanuvini
Colli Maceratesi, Bianco dei
Colli Morenici Mantovani
 del Garda
Colli Orientali del Friuli
Colli Tortonesi
Collio Goriziano
Conseil Petite Arvine,
 le Vin du
Cori Bianco
Cortese
Corvo
Costozza Riesling
Custoza, Bianco di
Devite
Dolce
Erbaluce di Caluso
Est! Est!! Est!!! di
 Montefiascone
Etna Bianco
Falerio dei Colli Ascolani
Franciacorta Pinot
Frascati
Frecciarossa
Friuli-Venezia-Giulia

Gabiola Bianco
Gambellara
Gavi
Gewürztraminer
Grave del Friuli
Greco di Bianco
Greco di Tufo
Gribianco
Ischia
Isonzo
Lachrima Christi
Latisana
Liquoroso
Locorotondo
Lugana
Malvasia
Malvasia di Bosa
Malvasia di Cagliari
Malvasia di Sardegna
Malvasia delle Lipari
Malvoisie de Nus
Marino
Martina or Martina Franca
Monsupello
Montecarlo
Montecompatri-Colonna
Monterosso Val d'Arda
Montonico
Moscato di Cagliari
Moscato di Noto
Moscato di Pantelleria
Moscato di Siracusa
Moscato di Sorso-Sennori
Moscato di Trani
Müller-Thurgau
Muscat
Muscat de Frontignan
Nasco di Cagliari

Nuragus di Cagliari
Oltrepò Pavese
Orvieto
Pagadebit di Bertinoro
Parrina Bianco
Passito
Passito di Chambave
Piave or Vini del Piave
Picolit
Pinot Bianco
Pinot Blanc
Pinot Gris
Pitigliano, Bianco di
Pomino Bianco
Prosecco di Conegliano-
   Valdobbiadene
Ravello Bianco
Recioto Bianco
Recioto di Soave
Regaleali
Reserve du Prieur
Riesling
Sauvignon
Secco
Soave
Solopaca
Sylvaner
Terlano
Tocai
Tocai di Lison
Tocai di San Martino della
   Battaglia
Torgiano Bianco
Torricella
Traminer
Trebbianino Val Trebbia
Trebbiano
Trebbiano d'Abruzzo

Trebbiano di Aprilia
Trebbiano de Romagna
Trentino
Ugni Blanc
Valdadige Bianco
Val d'Aosta
Valle Isarco
Velletri
Veltliner
Verdicchio
Verduzzo
Vergine Valdichiana, Bianco
Vermentino di Alghero
Vermentino di Berchidda
Vermentino di Gallura
Vermentino di Oristano
Vermentino di Savona
Vernaccia
Vernaccia di San Gimignano
Vespaiolo
Vin Santo
Vin Santo di Gambellara
Vino Bianco
Weissburgunder
Weisser Burgunder
Welschriesling
Zagarolo

New Zealand
   Müller-Thurgau
   Sémillon

Portugal
   Alcobaca
   Arubti
   Azeitão
   Bairrada
   Branco

Bucellas
Bussaco
Carcávelos
Dão
Moscatel Setubal
Muscat
Vinho Verde

Rumania
Cotnari
Dragasani
Murfatlar
Muskat Ottonel
Odobesti
Sauvignon

South Africa
Chenin Blanc
Constantia
Nederburg
Paarl
Sémillon
Steen

Spain
Abocado
Aguamurcia
Aguilar de la Frontera
Alella
Blanco
Cariñena
Dulce
Malvasia
Manzanilla
Montilla
Muscat
Perelada
Rioja

Rueda
Vino Blanco
Xarello

Switzerland
Abbayes, Clos des
Aigle
Arbalète, Clos de l'
Bienne (Biel)
Chablais
Chasselas
Côte, la
Dézaley
Elbling
Epesses
Ermitage
Faverges
Fendant
Geneva
Johannisberg
Knipperlé
Neuchâtel
Sylvaner
Ticino
Valais
Vaud
Visperterminen
Yverdon
Yvorne

United States
Aligoté
Almaden
Aurora Blanc
Beaulieu Vineyards (BV)
Beringer
Blanc de Noirs
Blanc Fumé

Botrytis Cinerea
Bruce Winery, David
Bully Hill Winery
California
Catawba
Caymus Vineyards
Chablis
Chalone Vineyards
Chappellet Vineyards
Chardonnay
Chasselas
Chateau Montelena
Chateau St. Jean
Chenin Blanc
Christian Brothers
Concannon Vineyard
Concord
Delaware
Diamond, or Moore's
   Diamond
Diana
Dry Creek Vineyard
Dutchess
Elbling
Elvira
Emerald Riesling
Finger Lakes
Flora
Folle Blanche
Frank, Dr. Konstantin
Freemark Abbey
French Colombard
Fu Jin
Gewürztraminer
Gold Seal
Green Hungarian
Grey Riesling
Hanzell Vineyards

Haut Sauterne
Heitz Cellars
Hock
Keuka Lake
Labrusca
Malvasia
Malvasia Bianca
Martini, Louis M.
Maryland
Masson, Paul
Mayacamas Vineyards
May Wine
Mirassou Vineyards
Missouri Riesling
Mondavi Winery, Robert
Montbray Wine Cellars
Monterey Vineyard
Monteviña
Moselle
Muscadine
Muscat
Muscat Alexandria
Muscat de Frontignan
Muskat Ottonel
New York
Niagara
Noah
Novitiate of Los Gatos
Ontario
Papagni Winery, Angelo
Parducci Wine Cellars
Pedroncelli Winery
Phelps Vineyard, Joseph
Pinot Blanc
Pinot Gris
Rhine Wine
Riesling
Ripley

St. Michel
San Martin Vineyard
Sauterne
Sauvignon Blanc
Sauvignon Vert
Scuppernong
Sémillon
Seyval Blanc
Simi Winery
Sonoma Vineyards
Spring Mountain
Stag's Leap Wine Cellars
Sterling Vineyards
Stonegate Winery
Stony Hill Vineyard
Sutter Home
Sylvaner
Ugni Blanc
Veedercrest Vineyards
Veltliner
Verdelet
Vergennes
Washington
Wente Brothers

White Pinot
White Riesling
Yakima Valley

Yugoslavia
Grk
Laški Riesling
Lutomer
Malvazija Istarska
Müller-Thurgau
Muskat Ottonel
Muskateller
Rajnai Grašvina
Rajnski Rizling
Renski Riesling
Renski Rizling
Sauvignon
Sémillon
Sipon
Tigrovomleko
Traminer
Welschriesling
Zilavka